Victoria Harbor.   Grand Trunk R. R. Station

VICTORIA HARBOUR

A Mill~Town Legacy

Barbaranne Boyer
&
Michael A. Boyer

THE BOSTON MILLS PRESS

Canadian Cataloguing in Publication Data

Boyer, Barbaranne, 1945—
    Victoria Harbour

Bibliography
ISBN 0-919783-69-4

1. Victoria Harbour (Ont.)—History.
2. Company towns—Ontario—Victoria Harbour—
History.   3. Victoria Harbour Lumber Company.
4. Waldie, John.   I. Boyer, Michael, 1958—   .
II. Title.

FC3099.V52B69 1988   971.3'17   C88-095299-7
F1059.5.V52B69 1988

© Barbaranne Boyer and Michael Boyer, 1989

Design by Leslie Macredie
Typesetting by Flynn Trade Typesetting, Cambridge
Printed by Ampersand, Guelph

Published by:
THE BOSTON MILLS PRESS,
132 Main Street,
Erin, Ontario
N0B 1T0
519-833-2407   fax 519-833-2195

American Association
for State and Local History
Award of Merit

Winners of the
Heritage Canada
Communications Award

The publisher wishes to acknowledge the financial assistance
of The Canada Council and the Ontario Arts Council.

Front Cover:

Our Son being loaded with lumber at Victoria Harbour
c.1880s.   —COURTESY TED BELCHER AND BILL BARR

Title Page:

Built in the late 1890s, Victoria Harbour Station once
stood where the IGA now stands. Photo c.1910. The
man in the centre is Station Master Robert McDowell.
Note the American spelling of the word "Harbor".
                              —COURTESY CHARLES HEELS

Back Cover:

The Hogg's Bay trestle, built in 1907-08. During both
world wars the trestle was patrolled by armed guards
to safeguard against sabotage. The speed limit on the
trestle was five miles per hour.
                              —COURTESY OF ANDREW BOYER

Contents

*Peter and Clara Boyer outside their home on William
Street c.1930s.* —COURTESY BOYER FAMILY

*Andrew, Donald and Edward Boyer. It must be Wash
Monday, judging by the clothes flapping in the breeze.*
—COURTESY BOYER FAMILY

Dedication

Clarence Sykes, Victoria Harbour, 1987.

WHAT BEGAN AS a genealogy of our father's family in the autumn of 1986 soon took on new meaning as we delved into our grandparents' life in the village around the turn of the century. Within a few short weeks we realized that the sleepy little village where we had spent all our summer vacations as children had a history far beyond what we had imagined. By the spring of 1987 we had collected more than one hundred old photographs, some quite rare, most of which were loaned to us by family members, village residents, and the Local Architectural Conservation Advisory Committee. Gradually the fascinating story of John Waldie's mill-town legacy began to unfold.

This book is dedicated to all the descendants of Peter and Clara Boyer of Victoria Harbour, and to all those residents past and present who contributed their old family photographs and memories. A sincere thanks to Clarence Sykes for his warm-hearted hospitality and colourful yarns about life in a mill town. And a very special thanks to Michael's wife, Yvonne Boyer, whose patience, good humour and Macintosh computer helped to make our work more enjoyable.

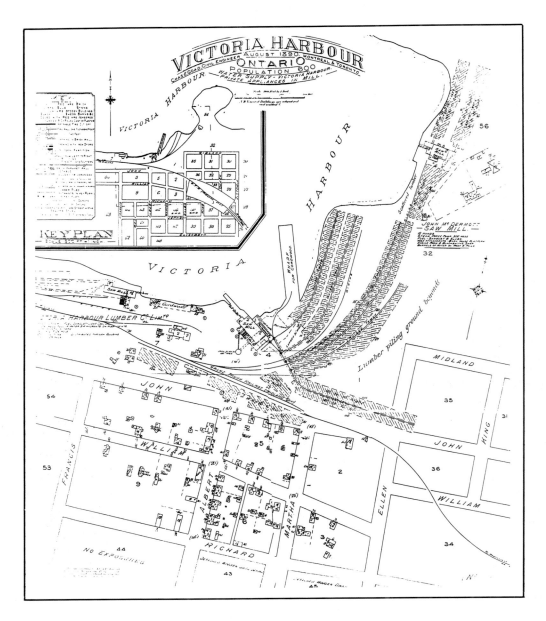

Acknowledgements

Clarence Sykes
  Victoria Harbour, Ontario

Stan and Helen Boyer
  Toronto, Ontario

Andrew and Vera Rumney Boyer
  Lindsay, Ontario

Art and Audrey Larmond
  Victoria Harbour, Ontario

Ken and Kay Pelletier
  Victoria Harbour, Ontario

Raymond G. Des Chenes
  Victoria Harbour, Ontario

Sue Murdock
  Simcoe County Archives,
  Midhurst, Ontario

Peter P. Moran, archivist
  Simcoe County Archives,
  Midhurst, Ontario

Catherine McKenzie
  Victoria Harbour, Ontario

Joseph Boyer
  Scarborough, Ontario

Don (Did) Cadeau,
  former fire chief
  Victoria Harbour, Ontario

Mr. and Mrs. Theo Burnard,
  owners IGA
  Victoria Harbour, Ontario

Tim O'Halloran
  Victoria Harbour, Ontario

Dwaine Moore
  Moore's Esso,
  Victoria Harbour, Ontario

Jean Moore
  Victoria Harbour, Ontario

Mrs. Lassiter
  Victoria Harbour, Ontario

Lorne Petroff
  Petroff Service Station,
  Victoria Harbour, Ontario

Jack LaChapelle
  Victoria Harbour, Ontario

Gerard LaChapelle
  Victoria Harbour, Ontario

Eugene and Violet Ladouceur
  Victoria Harbour, Ontario

Mrs. Marjory Eplett
  Victoria Harbour, Ontario

Mary Jarman
  Victoria Harbour, Ontario

Ted Belcher
  Victoria Harbour, Ontario

Celeste Larmond
  Victoria Harbour, Ontario

Wilfred Cote
  Victoria Harbour, Ontario

Lawrence and Debbie Horton
  Victoria Harbour, Ontario

Charles H. Heels
  Lindsay, Ontario

Eric Heels
  Midland, Ontario

Randy Childerhose
  Canadian Coast Guard,
  Parry Sound, Ontario

Alfie Yep
  Canadian Coast Guard,
  Toronto, Ontario

Dr. Richard Brown
  Canadian Archives,
  Ottawa, Ontario

Ken MacPherson
  Ontario Archives,
  Toronto, Ontario

Mrs. Vera Murray
  Georgian Manor,
  Midland, Ontario

Mr. and Mrs. Bob McDowell
  Victoria Harbour, Ontario

Lawrence and Barbara Barr
  Harbour Diner,
  Victoria Harbour, Ontario

Al Fortier
  Victoria Harbour, Ontario

Daniel Fortier
  Toronto, Ontario

Martha Bachtrog, clerk
  Village Office,
  Victoria Harbour, Ontario

Linda DesJardin, clerk
  Village Office,
  Victoria Harbour, Ontario

Donna Thatcher, clerk
  Village Office,
  Victoria Harbour, Ontario

Russel and Verna Reed
  Bobcaygeon, Ontario

Elizabeth Webb,
  public school secretary
  Victoria Harbour, Ontario

Ken and Lorraine Kitchen,
  photo reproduction
  Toronto, Ontario

Sue and Bill Duncan
  Photo Stop at the Beach,
  Toronto, Ontario

Father Philip, pastor
  St. Mary's Church
  Victoria Harbour, Ontario

(L to R) Walt Reid, Etta, Fred Eplett and Mrs. Eplett Sr.   —COURTESY MRS. EPLETT

Victoria Harbour
A Mill-Town Legacy

VICTORIA HARBOUR IS a peaceful, pleasant village cut off from the mainstream of traffic, by-passed by a highway and nestled in the crook of a sheltered bay.

On a warm autumn afternoon, from the top of the old lighthouse on the hill above the bay, one can see a rural countryside of farmland, meadows and tall forests ablaze in a glory of crimson and golds. To the west, above the treetops, you can see the twin spires of the Martyr's Shrine. Built in 1926, the Shrine overlooks the Wye River and Fort Ste. Marie in the Valley of the Saints.

To the east is the cupola of the Village Office, and beyond it Bergie's Point and Queen's Cove Marina, where elegant sailboats and pleasure craft bob on gentle swells in the harbour. Strung out along the shoreline from east to west are dozens of cottages and summer homes. To the north, across the bay, are the grain elevators at Port McNicoll, built in 1908 on land once known as Maple Island.

Southeast of the main crossroads of William and Albert streets are quiet, shady, tree-lined streets with charming clapboard cottages that date back nearly one hundred years, on and above William, on and off of Albert Street, are fashionable Victorian two-storey brick and rambling frame houses, all built around the turn of the century, most surrounded by wrap-around verandahs and shady back porches with ornate gingerbread trim. Neat lawns and gardens with picket fences and old-fashioned garden gates reflect the affluence and graceful charm of another era. Interspersed throughout the village are a growing number of modern new homes, evidence of revitalization.

West on William Street, a once graceful two-storey brick schoolhouse stands forlornly by the road, its doors and windows boarded up, its cupola and bell long since removed. Further along, on the corner of Albert Street, stands a splendid two-storey clapboard general store that dates back to 1902. On the opposite corner is a charming Victorian building topped with a cupola. The village library was housed here more than seventy-two years ago.

Every summer thousands of tourists make the trek north to visit the historic sites of Fort Ste. Marie and Martyr's Shrine near Midland, and the old Military and Naval Outpost at Penetanguishene. An atmosphere of hometown charm awaits tourists who leave the highway to pass through Victoria Harbour. But behind its quiet facade lies a wealth of history.

There was a time, centuries ago, when the lakes and rivers were pure, when densely wooded forests teemed with wildlife, when the Indians were the sole human inhabitants of this land.

Then the first explorers and voyageurs arrived from Quebec to map out this rugged terrain. A short time later the French Jesuit fathers took up residence along the banks of the river Wye, where they built their mission settlement among the Huron tribe. For one brief decade it flourished—until 1649, when the Iroquois captured hundreds of Hurons and two

Jesuit fathers. In defence, the Jesuits burned their mission and fled.

More than a century later, during the early days of the fur trade, a trading post was established at Penetanguishene. The early 1800s saw the construction of the region's first roads through Huronia, some following original Indian trails. Corduroy roads, rough and unyielding, were blazed through the forests. Built by the government of Upper Canada, the new thirty-five-mile military highway to its garrison on Penetanguishene Bay was completed in 1815.

After the War of 1812 the government issued its first Free Land Grants to ex-military men and United Empire Loyalists. By 1825 Governor Simcoe's Yonge Street road was finally linked with the Penetanguishene Road, providing a continuous route north from Toronto into Huronia.

The 1840s saw an influx of immigrant settlers lured to Ontario by correspondence from earlier settlers extolling the opportunities in this new country and by government Free Land Grant schemes. During this period thousands of Europeans left their homelands to begin new lives in central Ontario. Some travelled north by stagecoach or ox and wagon, others came aboard the schooners and steamers which plied the waters of Lake Simcoe and Georgian Bay. Most brought with them wooden crates and steamer trunks filled with both useful and frivolous items in preparation for their new beginning. Some brought their entire household furnishings, while many others arrived penniless, with little more than the clothes on their backs.

For many of those early pioneers, their first winter in Simcoe County was the hardest they had ever known. There were endless days of snow, floating silently down from a bland grey sky or arriving in fierce storms whipping in off the frozen bay and howling through the forests. Huddled under a thick blanket of ice and snow, the new settlers snuggled in their crude log cabins. Late arrivals sought shelter where they could and waited out the long, frigid nights until spring.

The 1850s and 60s saw many exciting innovations. New planked roads were being built throughout Ontario and the railroad had made its appearance. By the 1870s journeys north, which had previously taken days or even weeks of gruelling travel, could now be done in a day or two. At dizzying speeds steam engines rocked and swayed over hundreds of miles of new steel rail, pulling behind them a string of freight cars and coaches through dark, mossy forest, over wooden bridges spanning rivers and creeks, past log farmsteads and cleared fields. Settlers came north in search of a better life, travellers came in search of adventure, and tradesmen in search of new business.

As far as the eye could see, great stands of virgin white pine covered most of Simcoe County. And then the lumbermen came too. Sawmills sprang up along the banks of rivers and bay inlets, for suddenly there were fortunes to be made from the forests. Soon hundreds of logging camps dotted the woodlands and great falls of precious white pine and hardwood were sent cascading down deep, narrow gorges, past lush stands of maple and towering oak, into the windswept waters of Georgian Bay.

It was in the 1830s that an ex-military man named John Hogg first settled along the banks of the river west of the present-day village of Victoria Harbour and built perhaps one of the area's first sawmills. Gradually, as a settlement grew up around the mill, the area took on the name Hogg, as did the river and the bay.

By 1853 the McNabbs were operating on the abandoned ruins of Hogg's mill site, and by 1869 Albert Fowlie and John Kean, businessmen from Orillia, along with Richard Power and W. D. Ardough from Barrie, had purchased land in the vicinity. They built up an extensive sawmill operation to the east of

Hogg River and called it Kean and Fowlie and Company. The sawmill operated until 1876.

During those early days on Hogg's Bay several other mills flourished for a time. They included the Nickerson Brothers Mills, John McDermott's mill, and the Power Lumber Company. In the 1870s and 80s tall-masted sailing ships frequently called at Victoria Harbour to load lumber heading for ports in Canada and the United States. Today, if you drive south through Detroit to Cincinnati on US I-75, you will see hundreds of wooden houses, all framed, rafted, floored

A familiar scene out on the frozen bay at Victoria Harbour c.1900.
—COURTESY EUGENE AND VIOLET LADOUCEUR

and shingled with lumber from our Georgian Bay mills.

The barge *Vanderbilt* was a familiar sight on Hogg's Bay in the 1870s, as was the sailing ship *Our Son*. As more new settlers moved into the area, the village grew. In July 1872 the first official post office was established east of the river and was christened Victoria Harbour, in honour of the reigning queen.

The timely arrival of Scottish entrepreneur John Waldie in 1885 brought a welcome new vitality to the little village. By 1911, the year of incorporation, Victoria Harbour boasted a population of well over two thousand, making it the largest village in Simcoe County.

During those golden years Victoria Harbour seemed to epitomize the growth and prosperity of the lumber industry in Ontario. New buildings were

An aerial view of the village and the mills c.1918-19 (looking east). Note the school in the lower left corner.
—COURTESY LACAC

going up everywhere and every day more new faces appeared on the streets. In that golden era the village, like the country as a whole, radiated optimism. They could boast of a fine two-storey brick bank building, two silent movie theatres, the Gem and the Crystal, and two hotels, the Queen's and the Royal Victoria. There was a weekly newspaper called the *New Era*, a resident photographer, a doctor, a pharmacist, a bakery, a cafe, a billiards hall, and ice-cream parlours. There were several general and dry goods stores, and a butcher shop, as well as blacksmiths' and livery stables. There were three churches, a school, a Masonic Temple, an Orange Hall, and down by the bay an impressive new railway station. But most importantly, there was a major employer—John Waldie's Victoria Harbour Lumber Company.

Aerial view of Albert Street (looking north). In the lower left corner is the roof of Waldie's ice rink, reputed to be the largest indoor rink north of Toronto. Clearly visible are the mills, the station, the hotel, the library and the old company store.
—COURTESY LACAC

John Waldie, president, Victoria Harbour Lumber Company.

John Waldie and the Victoria Harbour Lumber Company

THE CARRIAGE ROLLED quietly through the streets of the sleepy village as daylight was dawning. At the main crossroads of William and Albert streets it drew to a halt. From his vantage point John Waldie keenly surveyed the scene. To his right, along William Street, were his millworkers' cottages, painted yellow with neat, whitewashed picket fences surrounding them, and on the hill above Ellen Street stood the newly completed Presbyterian Church, a quaint edifice, his gift to the village. On the southeast corner stood the Bank of Toronto and the shops of the village merchants, all fronted by rough planked boardwalks. Across the dirt road was the company store and behind it, on Albert Street, the company offices. Waldie could see the three-storey frame Royal Victoria Hotel, with its neat lawns and flowering shrubs, and the carriage house behind it.

On this quiet Sabbath morning the sun streamed brightly across the waters of the bay, casting its golden flashes off the windows of the brick powerhouse and washing its warm glow over the slumbering village.

At age seventy-three John Waldie had reason to feel complacent, for among his many extensive holdings the Victoria Harbour Lumber Company was a source of pride and he took pleasure in the familiar sights around him. Out on the bay booms of logs filled the harbour, and down along the wharf, at the foot of Albert Street, every description of craft bobbed in the water—steamers, tugs and fishing boats—all secured in the early morning hours. To the east he could see his lumberyards and railsidings, where great pyramids of raw cut lumber stood waiting for shipment, its fresh scent wafting in the air. He could see the one-hundred-foot iron wood-burners, the railway station and his three mills, which together produced more than 200,000 board feet of lumber a day. Yes, he'd worked hard these past twenty years. The business world called him a philanthropist and an entrepreneur, a man of many talents, a lumber baron whose company had become the second-largest milling operation in Canada and third-largest in North America.

John Waldie was born April 22, 1833, at Hawick, Scotland, and immigrated to Canada with his parents, James and Jessie Waldie, while still a young boy. The family settled at Burlington in Halton County, and it was here that John Waldie began his business career as a merchant. At age twenty-six he married Miss Mary Thompson of Halton. Over the next twenty-five years he prospered. During that time he also launched a political career, first as Reeve of Burlington for five years, followed by another two years as Reeve of Nelson Township.

After the death of his wife in 1884 Waldie prepared to make the move to Toronto. His children, seven sons and six daughters, were grown and no longer required his attention. At the age of fifty-two, when most men might be considering their retirement, John Waldie was only just beginning.

The following year he purchased the Power Lumber Company at Victoria Harbour in Simcoe County. His first mill was located east of Hogg River and would become known as No. 1 mill. Next he bought out Keane and Fowlie and Company's mill situated at the foot of Albert Street. This mill was called No. 2 mill and was destroyed by fire in 1918. The original powerhouse was also located on this site. The plant not only provided power for the mills but also the company store, the offices and the Royal Victoria Hotel. In 1900 Waldie purchased John McDermott's mill on Bergie's Point, and here he reconstructed a mill brought up from Fenelon Falls, Ontario. This mill was No. 3 mill, and a new power plant was built here after the 1918 fire.

No. 3 mill was the most modern of his mills, with a gang-saw that had the capacity to saw twenty-four logs simultaneously, spewing out more than half a boxcar load of boards at once. There was also a dry kiln, a machine shop, a shingle and planing mill. The company's piling yards extended to Park Street opposite the cemetery. For ten hours a day, six days a week, the steady whine of saws echoed through the village and across the bay, trains shunted back and forth in the yards, and more than fifty carloads of cut lumber left town each day.

Because of the size of the mill, a large

Mill No. 1 c.1890.

—PHOTO H. L. GARDINER, COURTESY ONTARIO ARCHIVES

The remains of pilings from No. 1 mill c.1930s. In the background (L to R) are the Royal Victoria Hotel, the company office and the railway station.

—COURTESY MRS. EPLETT

Mill No. 3 at Bergie's Point c.1900.
—PHOTO H. L. GARDINER,
COURTESY ONTARIO ARCHIVES

*Interior view of one of the company's
mills c.1890.* —COURTESY LACAC

Millworkers posing at the mill c.1900. It wasn't unusual for boys as young as ten to be employed on the boardway.
—COURTESY CLARENCE SYKES

population was required to run it efficiently: mill-wrights, sawyers, loggers, millhands, yard and dock workers, office staff, clerks, bookkeepers, stable hands, foremen and managers.

After the purchase of the Power Lumber Company in 1885, construction began on the first of the millworkers' homes, in addition to a single men's boarding house. When these were completed the company was able to advertise for men in newspapers as far away as New York state and Quebec. Ready accommodation, the promise of job security and a steady paycheque were enough to lure both single men and those with families up to Simcoe County. By the late 1880s men were lining up for jobs in the mills and more new housing had to be provided.

It was a common practice for owners of large milling operations to provide for their employees. It was typical for a man to live in a company house, buy his goods from the company store, and participate in social activities organized by the company. Waldie's mill town was like those south of the border. While the mills at Harris and Hampton, Rhode Island, and Harrisville in New Hampshire were textile mills, the concept was the same. The construction of mills was followed by the building of company-owned houses, a boarding house, offices, a company store, a church, a library and often a school. It is quite possible that Mr. Waldie toured mill towns throughout New England to see their layout and design first-hand before planning his own. Early mill houses were built to provide low-cost housing for large numbers of people. Although their designs were based purely on economics, their simplicity added to their appeal.

In Victoria Harbour all the buildings were wood-frame structures of one-and-a-half or two-storey designs. The first to be built were the quaint clapboard cottages similar in design to the American "salt box." These were followed by the "terrace house," six units under one roof with a full-length verandah along the front. This unique townhouse was demolished in the late 1930s. Next came the "double house," and finally a particular design of home reserved for company managers. These houses were single-family dwellings, two storeys with wrap-around verandahs and bay windows.

While both millworkers' homes and commercial buildings connected with the company remained quite conservative in their architecture, there seemed to be some thoughts of grandeur in the design of the imposing powerhouse, built around 1890. This beautifully proportioned red brick structure featured an unusual two-storey brick tower with a two-storey mansard roof topped with an ornate iron finial. This powerhouse was the only brick building to be constructed by the Victoria Harbour Lumber Company. All other buildings, including the company store, were painted in the company colours, a bright yellow with white trim.

At its peak the company employed more than five hundred workers. The general welfare of these people came under the "paternal system," with the Victoria Harbour Lumber Company as self-appointed head of the community, for almost everyone was in some way or another connected with the mills. No doubt there were those who sorely resented what they saw as a dictatorship in kind, but for the most part the majority welcomed the security of life in a mill town, where a sense of well-being and camaraderie prevailed.

Millworkers' homes on Albert Street (facing southeast) c.1890. These homes were designed along the lines of the American "salt box." Twelve years after this photograph was taken, the lot to the left became the site of the Royal Victoria Hotel. The house on the corner became the home of the village library in 1916.

—COURTESY LACAC

The Terrace House was built by the Victoria Harbour Lumber Company on the south side of Jephson Street between King and Queen streets in the 1890s. The building contained six units. It was torn down in the late 1930s. Note the unusual lighter shading above the roof line of the verandah.
—COURTESY LACAC

One of the original village houses.
—PHOTO MICHAEL A. BOYER

This house on Bay Street is a charming example of a typical turn-of-the-century home. Nearly every house had a garden plot and a fence surrounding it.
—COURTESY CLARENCE SYKES

The powerhouse in 1906 with engine No. 1 passing by.
—PHOTO H. L. GARDINER, COURTESY ONTARIO ARCHIVES

One of the many houses built by the Victoria Harbour Lumber Company for their foremen and department heads. This one on Jephson Street still stands, minus the picket fence.
—COURTESY MRS. EPLETT

The home of Philip Schissler, former Victoria Harbour resident and foreman at the lumber company. This house on Richard Street still stands.

—COURTESY THEO BERNARD

It was a practice during those early years for Mr. Waldie to present the parents of every male child born in the village with a five-dollar gold piece, and at Christmas each family received a large turkey. What profited the company benefited the village as a whole.

The company owned and operated four tugs, the *Charlton*, the *Lily*, the *Reginald*, and the *Superior*. They had a grain ship called the *Tadousoc*, which was later sold to the Canada Steamship Lines. Waldie's yacht, the *Siesta*, was used for coast guard duty during the First World War and afterwards proudly displayed a star on her stack for sinking a German submarine.

Situated on the southwest side of Albert Street, near the bottom of the hill, were the company stables, where great Clydesdales were kept. During the winter months both horses and men left for logging camps up north to cut timber for the mills.

The great flurry of construction which took place between 1886 and 1900 continued into the new century. In 1902 a new company office was nearing completion across the road from the boarding house on Albert Street when a fire broke out in the furnace room at the men's residence and sparks from the blaze quickly ignited the roof of the office. Despite the efforts of the mill, village and Midland fire brigades, both buildings were totally levelled. Within two months after the fire, construction crews were working six days a week rebuilding the office and a new

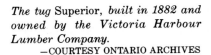

The tug Superior, *built in 1882 and owned by the Victoria Harbour Lumber Company.*
—COURTESY ONTARIO ARCHIVES

combination boarding house and hotel.

The Royal Victoria Hotel proved to be a definite advantage to the village, which was now attracting tourists to the area. The spawling three-storey Victorian-style hotel was first-class in all its appointments. Its interior was furnished in oak, as was the staircase and wainscot panelling. Fine prints and paintings covered the walls, and fern stands and horsehair armchairs were set upon Axminster rugs, lending an air of refinement to the new hotel.

The dining room was just as gracious, with white linen-covered tables and oak sideboards set with china tea services and silver platters. There was also a private dining room for the exclusive use of the men who boarded in rooms in the back of the hotel. Outside, a wide full-length verandah offered guests a good spot to view the comings and goings along the harbourfront. Due to the temperance of its owner, the Royal Victoria Hotel absolutely prohibited spirits of any kind on its premises, and it wasn't until the forties that liquor was served there.

For more than half a century the Royal Victoria was a landmark in the village, but with the demise of the lumber company in 1927 and the depression that followed, the old hotel gradually fell into disuse. By 1961, the year it was razed by fire, the Royal Victoria Hotel was virtually a derelict building.

John Waldie's foresight paid off. Prior to his death Waldie purchased the timber rights and mills of Cook and Brothers Lumber Company at Spragg, Ontario, for two million dollars, followed by the million-dollar purchase of the Eddy Timber limits on Lake Penage. Who would have believed that within twenty-five years the timber limits would run out?

On June 12, 1907, at his home, "Glenhurst" in the Rosedale section of Toronto, John Waldie passed away. At the time of his death Mr. Waldie was president of the Landed Banking and Loan Company of Hamilton, and president of the Magnetawan Tanning and Electric Company, and Toby Limited of Collingwood, both leather concerns. He was the director of the Bank of Toronto and the Toronto Paper Coating Mill Limited. He also had a number of other smaller enterprises. It was written of John Waldie in Canadian Biography: "He was the exceptional type of country merchant who, at middle age, enters a large arena and by the experience he has gained, and by combining honesty with shrewdness, has reaped a great fortune."

John Waldie left a lasting legacy in Victoria Harbour. The picturesque little village built on the bay is dotted here and there with a good number of well-preserved Victorian-style buildings which owe their construction to Waldie. The village of Victoria Harbour has been through several economic phases. Once a thriving mill town, it survived the closing of its mills and the gradual decline in its population, even the Depression. Today the village is on the rebound. Its residents are busy restoring their properties, and the village Local Architectural Conservation Advisory Committee (LACAC) is actively working to restore its public buildings. Tourism is taking over as the primary industry, and because of its location and its size, the village is also appealing to city dwellers looking for an escape from the hustle and bustle of larger centres and willing to commute in exchange for a more tranquil lifestyle.

The Victoria Hotel and boarding house was built by the Victoria Harbour Lumber Company in the autumn of 1902 after a fire destroyed the original boarding house on March 27 of that year. Some old-timers fondly recall that the hotel lawn had "the best damn dew-worms in town." This photo c.1907.
—COURTESY THEO BERNARD

This 1956 photograph of the Victoria Hotel was taken in the building's final days. The old hotel burned down in 1961. Opposite is the Victoria Harbour Lumber Company office, also built in 1902 and the victim of fire in 1958.
—COURTESY ANDREW BOYER

The Boyer Home was built in 1900 and still stands, minus its verandah, on the west end of William Street. This photo c.1940s. Older residents can recall times when the snow was so deep you had to climb out a second-storey window to leave the house.
   —COURTESY KAY PELLETIER

Gasoline launch used by Peter Boyer c.1919.
   —COURTESY JOSEPH BOYER

Mr. and Mrs. Job Smyth c.1890s. Mr. Smyth was a contractor for the lumber company.
—COURTESY MISS C. McKENZIE

"Say cheese!"—obviously no one did back then. Hogg's Bay c.1920s.
—COURTESY AUDREY LARMOND

Grandad's hunting party c.1920s. Good times and even better memories.
—COURTESY MRS. VERA BOYER

The old Dutton Hunt Club heading home c.1930. Do you recognize anyone on this South Magnetawan station platform?
—COURTESY MRS. VERA BOYER

Fabian and Marie LaChappelle on their wedding day c.1920s   —COURTESY OF AUDREY LARMOND

Frederick Norval Waldie

FREDERICK WALDIE WAS born in Burlington, Ontario, on April 8, 1875, and was educated at Upper Canada College. At the age of nineteen Fred began his career in the Victoria Harbour Lumber Company on the bottom rung as a minor employee. He worked his way up through the ranks, learning the various phases of the lumber industry in preparation for the day when he would succeed his father. Through the years of his apprenticeship he gained a broad working knowledge of the conditions and problems associated with the business. Following his father's death in 1907 he stepped in with apt ability and leadership

Like his father, Fred Waldie proved himself to be a worthy businessman. He also took part in both political and civic endeavours. He was a devoted member of the Presbyterian Church and a generous supporter of worthy charities. He took a genuine interest in the village and was active both in his mills and socially. In 1905 he organized a hockey team which put the village on the map after winning the Ontario Intermediate Championship that very first year. Throughout Simcoe County the team was referred to as "the boys from sawdust town." In 1916 he built a new library.

After the death of his first wife, Frances Heron, the niece of the Hon. George Brown, Waldie married again. His second wife, Florence Margaret, passed away in April 1927, leaving one daughter, Margaret Norval Waldie. Four months later, on August 27, 1927, the same year the lumber company shut down, Fred Waldie died suddenly at the Waldie summer residence at Woodland, Shanty Bay. His passing was a great loss to those who knew him privately and in the business world. He left a large sum of money to be divided among the needy families of those employed by his lumber company, as well as a monetary gift to St. Paul's on the hill in the village.

John Waldie's eldest son, James William, married Miss Sarah Susanah Vasey at Allendale in 1893 and later was involved in mining in British Columbia. Another son, Robert S., became a member of the law firm Meredith, Cameron and Waldie. Two other brothers were engaged in the lumber business in Toronto. During the First World War his sons Charles Percival and W. Scott Waldie served overseas. Charles Percival was killed in action in the Loos Drive at Arras in 1915 and Major W. Scott Waldie, a member of a Muskoka regiment, died in Wales while awaiting transportation home after the close of the war.

Engineer Charlie Schissler sits at the controls of a snowed-in yard engine c.1920s. —COURTESY CLARENCE SYKES

Early Days of Railroading

THE YEAR WAS 1878 and the Midland Railway of Canada had just finished laying their new line from Orillia through Medonte to the village of Waubaushene on the shores of Georgian Bay.

The arrival of the summer season in Victoria Harbour the following year also brought the "iron horse" to the village. On July 14, 1879, the Midland Railway Company extended the line from Waubaushene through Victoria Harbour to the village of Midland, thus connecting the village and its people to the rest of the province. Prior to the arrival of the railroad, goods and mail were shipped to Waubaushene and dispatched to the Georgian Bay villages by the steamer *Myrtie*.

With the arrival of the railway, lumbering possibilities increased in the area. By the end of the 1880s the Victoria Harbour Lumber Company had built rail sidings off the main line to their No. 1 and No. 2 mills, and later to No. 3 mill. Servicing the yard were two company-owned yard engines, or as they were more commonly known "dinky engines" or "saddle tanks."

One practice Waldie had was to stamp the side of each and every car of lumber leaving the yard with V.H.L.C. This practice continued for some time, until the Grand Trunk Railway put a stop to it, saying it was free advertising for the lumber company.

One of the Victoria Harbour Lumber Company yard engines, commonly known as "dingy engines" c.1890.
—COURTESY ONTARIO ARCHIVES

Railroad excursions became very popular in the 1890s. The railroaders between Midland and Orillia would all join together on a special train leaving Midland early in the morning and stopping at Victoria Harbour, Waubaushene and other small villages along the line on their way to the park in Orillia for a day's outing with fellow workers and family.

In August 1906 one of the few accidents ever to occur in Victoria Harbour blocked the main line to Midland for several days. It was on a hot, sunny August day when Conductor J. MacMillan and Engineer Lewis Gordon were switching into the west lumberyard of the V.H.L.C. after the train had moved off the main line and into the mill. The brakeman forgot to switch back to the main line, leaving two stub ends of rail leading to nowhere. However the brakeman did set the west semaphore to the stop position to protect trains approaching from the west. Meanwhile engineers Bill Hearst and George Hayes, both of Allendale, had just departed from the Midland elevators with twenty thirty-ton boxcars loaded with flaxseed. As the freight train approached Victoria Harbour the two men failed to notice the semaphore and ran by it. They also failed to notice that the passing

DERAILMENT - VICTORIA HARBOR - AUGUST 1906.

The wreck of the 164 and the 285 just west of the station at Victoria Harbour in 1906.
—COURTESY CHARLES HEELS

track switch was set against them. When they did finally notice, it was too late to stop. The two engines and seven boxcars ran out of track and bounced along the ties, coming to rest in a heap of metal and flaxseed.

After the Grand Trunk Railway investigation, the two engineers were discharged and other members of the two crews, including the brakeman, received suspensions without pay. That was very serious punishment back in the early days because payday came only once a month, wages were low and what little money they made had to stretch over a long period of time.

In 1907 the Canadian Pacific Railway started operations near Victoria Harbour. C.P.R. owned and operated the grain elevator in Port McNicoll, along with several steam passenger ships on the Great Lakes. CP.R. ran mostly freight trains out of Port McNicoll, but also ran a special train out of Toronto called the "boat train." Passengers would board in Toronto for the trip to Port McNicoll, where they would disembark and board one of the company-owned passenger ships for a cruise along the Great Lakes.

In 1922, under Sir Henry Worth Thornton, Canadian National Railway took control of the Grand Trunk Railway, and a new era of railroading began in Canada. By the end of 1927 the Victoria Harbour Lumber Company had shut down its mills. The buildings were eventually torn down and the rail sidings removed. The railroad continued to service the village with freight and passenger service until the mid-1960s, when the station was torn down by the railroad.

The old Park Street bridge, built in 1879.
—COURTESY MRS. EPLETT

Waiting for the train c.1920s. Charles Vent and Jim Gill smile for the camera on the platform of the old Victoria Harbour railway station. —COURTESY MRS. EPLETT

The Town Depot

DURING THE MIDDLE of the nineteenth century, railroad track was laid throughout Ontario. Small villages were constructed along the steel rails, houses were built, businesses were opened and communities were started.

One building that was built in every town along the railroad doubled as a business and meeting place. That building was the town's railroad station or depot. In the early days of railroading the depot was the centre of activity. Knowing this, the railroad companies went to great lengths to build large, attractive, impressive-looking structures.

On July 14, 1879, Midland Railway track was laid through Victoria Harbour, and by the end of that year the village's first depot was built. Built in batten-board design, this structure was not as impressive as the depot to follow, but did have a character of its own, from its small, arched windows to the unique woodwork in its waiting room.

This smaller depot served the village for some eighteen years before being replaced in the late 1890s with a larger stucture just down the track. This new structure, also in the batten-board design, was one hundred feet long and twenty-four feet wide. On one end of the building was one of the two large bay windows, and on the other end stood the freight shed, with its large sliding freight door facing the wooden-planked platform that stretched the length of the station. The whole exterior of the station was painted a two-tone brown, dark brown on the bottom half and light brown on the top, with all the decorative trim painted the same dark brown.

The interior of the station was just as impressive, lit by oil lamps and heated by a wood stove. The waiting room was the centre of activity, with pine floors and wainscotting throughout. The walls and ceilings were painted white and the trim a light brown. On the walls hung colourful railway posters, a map of the railway system, the local timetable, and of course

Victoria Harbour's first depot (off-centre right), built in 1879. No. 2 mill (top).

the regulation clock. Wooden benches lined the walls and a large wood stove sat in the centre, usually with a pot of coffee brewing on it.

The ticket office, with its arched window, was just inside the front door. Here passengers purchased tickets and checked baggage. The interior of the ticket and station master's office was typical of most stations. At the ticket window sat the ticket box and dater. On the agent's mahogany desk sat a blotter, an assortment of stamps and brass baggage checks. On another desk was the telegraph machine (later to be replaced by the scissors phone). On the back wall hung a large GT.R. calendar along with an assortment of keys hanging from nails.

In the freight shed boxes and crates lined the walls, extra hand lanterns hung from the rafters and a large weigh scale sat in the middle of the room near the freight door.

In the early days they were known as station masters, station agents, depot agents and even masters of the depot. One man who was resposible for the upkeep and operation of the station was Robert N. McDowell. Born in Milton, Ontario, in 1873, Robert first found employment with the Grand Trunk Railway in Milton and became the town's station master on October 29, 1889. He held this position until approx-imately 1896-7, when the new station was built in Victoria Harbour. At that time he was transferred here and became the station's first agent.

The station master's duties were many in the early days of railroading. They consisted of selling tickets, handling baggage, setting the order board, sweeping the floors, even doing double duty as the telegraph operator. In 1901 Robert married sixteen-year-old Nellie Salbows of Victoria Harbour. They lived on William Street, a stone's throw from the station. Robert continued as station master for over forty years. In 1915 Robert was twenty-second on the G.T.R. seniority list.

By the early 1920s eight to ten trains rambled through the village daily. A new oil-and-electric train was in service on the line at that time. After the mills closed down in 1927, passenger and freight service continued.

In 1939 Robert retired from the railroad at the age of sixty-six. Two years later, Station Master Robert N. McDowell died. The station continued to operate until finally the railroad was forced to cancel passenger and freight service in the 1960s. The station was torn down in the late sixties. The iron horse had been replaced by the automobile.

Station Master Robert McDowell and his wife, Nelly. Robert McDowell was the first station master at Victoria Harbour. He retired in 1939.
—COURTESY McDOWELL FAMILY

JBR/EB

ADDRESS REPLY TO
DEPUTY MINISTER
OF MARINE AND FISHERIES,
OTTAWA.
REFER TO NO. 22017X1-X

Ottawa 31st May, 1912.

Sir,

     I have to inform you that by Order-in-Council of the 24th May, 1912, you have been appointed keeper of the light at Victoria Harbour, Ontario, to fill the vacancy caused by the death of Mr. Charles Berzie; your salary to be at the rate of $180. per annum, rising by annual increments of $10 subject to good behaviour and efficient service, to a maximum of $220. per annum, dating from the time on which you took charge of the light.

Enc.

     The accompanying form relating to date of birth, etc., be good enough to fill in and return to the Department.

     I am, Sir,

       Your obedient servant,

       Assistant Deputy Minister.

Mr. Robert Belcher,
   Lightkeeper,
     VICTORIA HARBOUR, ONT.

Lighthouses

IT WAS IN the early nineteenth century that lighthouses started to appear on Ontario's shorelines, but it wasn't until 1857-58 that light started to shine on Georgian Bay.

With the opening of the C.P.R.'s grain terminal in Port McNicoll in 1908 and the increased ship traffic in the area from both C.P.R.'s cruise ships and V.H.L.C.'s lumber freighters, an aid to navigation was needed. After much research, two range lights were built in the village in 1910 by the Public Works, with G. Dobson of Victoria Harbour as project foreman. The two structures cost $1,766.81 to construct and took over six months to complete.

One lighthouse was erected near the shoreline on Bergie's Point and the other was positioned on the hill overlooking William near the public school. Both ranges were fixed red lights.

On October 15, 1910, the kerosene wicks were lit for the first time by the first lighthouse keeper, Charles Burzie of Victoria Harbour. Charles kept the lights for two years before resigning in 1912. In May 1912, after receiving a letter of appointment from the Assistant Deputy Minister, Robert Belcher, also of the village, became the second lighthouse keeper, with an annual salary of $180. Tragedy struck soon after, however, when Robert died of cholera on July 10 of that same year.

The development of kerosene or mineral oil in the late 1800s by Dr. Abraham Gesner greatly improved the quality of light. Before kerosene, whale sperm and seal oil were used in lighthouses as a source of fuel. Once a month Dominion steamers would deliver fuel and supplies to the various lighthouses on Georgian Bay. In Victoria Harbour all supplies were delivered to the light on Bergie's Point.

Upon Robert's death his brother Ray took over as third lighthouse keeper. Ray looked after the lights until he was shipped overseas to fight the war. During the war years Clarence Sykes kept the light, and when Ray returned in 1918 he resumed his position as keeper. Ray continued to maintain the lights until 1951, when the lighthouses were switched over to electric power.

In June 1960 the lighthouse on Bergie's Point was torn down and replaced with a skeleton steel tower with the fixed red light atop. In that same year, Ray Belcher, the man who had watched over the old lighthouse for forty years, died.

The last keeper was W. B. Cooke, who ran the lights intil 1968, when Canadian Coast Guard Base Parry Sound took over operation of the lighthouse.

In September 1985 the rear lighthouse underwent major renovations. The entire structure was strengthened and aluminum siding was installed. Today the red-and-white lighthouse still operates, guiding ships into the safety of the harbour, a tradition for over seventy-five years.

Lighthouse keeper Ray Belcher poses in front of Bergie's Point lighthouse c.1920s.
—COURTESY TED BELCHER

The Victoria Harbour Hockey Team

IN 1904 CONSTRUCTION began on a new indoor ice arena located on Albert Street near Maple. Waldie's Rink, as it was soon known, was reputed to be the largest indoor rink north of Toronto and also home to the newly formed Victoria Harbour Hockey Club. Organized by Victoria Harbour Lumber Company owner Fred Waldie, the team was largely made up of lumber company employees.

The team began their first season in 1905, playing in the O.H.A. Intermediate League. In that same year the "sawdust town boys" astounded the countryside by winning the Intermediate Championship. It was a jubilant time for the team, Fred Waldie, and the village as a whole, as it was the first time that the championship had ever been won by a club from this part of Ontario.

The team members included: E. Switzen, centre; E. Drolet, left wing; G. Goode, right wing; Con Corbeau, point; M. Goodwin, cover; H. Corbeau, cover; J. McLaughlin, spare; D'Arcy Regan, goal; S. Burns, mascot. The team executive members included: Fred Waldie, honorary president; R. Henderson, vice-president; J. A. Eplett, president; R. J. Grimes, manager; Wm. Steward, manager; J. Duckworth, secretary-treasurer; G. Vent, T. Brown, P. Ball, P. Schissler, committee.

Waldie's Rink served the community for over fifteen years. It also served as a training centre for soldiers during World War I, before succumbing to fire in 1922.

The Victoria Harbour Men's Hockey Team, photographed at Gardiner's Studio c.1910. Recognize anyone?
—COURTESY LACAC

The Victoria Harbour Boys' Hockey Team c.1920s: (L to R top) Clarence Sykes, Johnny McNab, Lorne Eplett, Charlie Jackson; (L to R bottom) Ken MacDonald, Charlie Lumson, Mr. Fallis, George Malcom and Wilfred Stoddard. —COURTESY CLARENCE SYKES

Mark Vasey and the Village Post Office

MARK VASEY WAS born in Rillington, Yorkshire, England, on November 28, 1843, and immigrated to the colonies with his family as a lad of ten. After spending their first two years in Montreal the family moved to Ontario, settling in Medonte Township.

Several years later a young Mark Vasey opened a general store in the front part of his log home, where later the first post office was established. A settlement grew up around the post office and soon took on the name Vasey. At the age of thirty-three Mr. Vasey was appointed postmaster at Victoria Harbour, a position he held for thirty-nine years. During the ensuing years he also held a variety of other positions, including station agent for the Midland Railway in 1879 and from 1880-81 assessor for Tay Township.

He was a community-spirited man and a licensed preacher in the Methodist Church, conducting services at both Victoria Harbour and Ebenezer. He was also superintendent of the Sunday School, as well as the choir leader.

In 1910 the congregation presented him with a handsome chair in honour of his dedication to the church and community. On November 7, 1915, Mark Vasey died suddenly at Victoria Harbour. His wife, Elizabeth, took over as village postmistress for several years, conducting business out of their home on Richard Street.

Vasey house, Victoria Harbour.

49

The Victoria Harbour Post Office

George Pawley - shopkeeper, 1872 first postmaster
Mark Vasey - March 1876-1915
Jim Sykes - rural route carrier 1900
Elizabeth Vasey - 1915-26
Clark Nicols - 1926-28
Archie Thorburn - June 1928
Philip Morrow - 1928-April 1956
Ken Pelletier - 1956-1965
Rod Steele - 1965-1972
Robert Colbourne - 1972-1983
Clara Pelletier - 1983 to present

Mark and Elizabeth Vasey.
—COURTESY MRS. EPLETT

The Village Library

IN THE 1890s an organized women's movement called "The Women's Christian Temperance Union" rallied around the prohibition issue. Alcohol was a particular concern in Victoria Harbour because of its large male population of millworkers. More than one lumber company accident, including fires, was attributed to "hard spirits." John Waldie and later his son Fred, both staunch Presbyterians, were advocates of temperance. The Royal Victoria Hotel and boarding house was dry, leaving millworkers to find "release" from hard work and boredom through homemade brew or a pint across the bar at the Queen's Hotel. With a work force made up of many imported labourers, including native Indians, French Canadians, Irish, Scots, and other Europeans, many of whom had no real permanent roots in the village, the problem appeared to be a sufficient one. In 1914 Fred Waldie actively lobbied for a pro-prohibition vote in the village, and it appears that the new library was his "gift" for a NO vote.

An architectural gem, the library was built on the northeast corner of William and Albert streets in 1915. The one-and-a-half-story clapboard building featured a steep cedar-shingled roof topped with a charming cupola. The stone foundation was built by a local mason named Joseph Evans. During its construction Mr. Waldie often came to the worksite to inspect its progress. The original interior boasted high-ceilinged reading rooms, with a handsome fireplace in each one, finely crafted wood panelling, and tall windows which allowed for shafts of light even on dreary days. Upon its completion in 1916 Fred Waldie presented the library to the village. The first appointed librarian was Miss O'Donahue, followed by Miss Lana Gouett.

Ten years later the library, as such, ceased to exist, and for many years the building stood vacant. In 1932, following the fire which destroyed the business block on the southwest corner of the main streets, village photographer Douglas Robertson and his family took up residence in the building, and he operated his business from that location until 1943. For another three years it remained empty, until 1946-47, when the Victoria Chemical Company occupied it.

In 1948 the Victoria Harbour and Tay Township offices became the last residents. During the fifties extensive restoration work was done. When the old false ceiling was removed, workers discovered two cups hidden away, one silver and one pewter, along with a copy of an old *New Era* newspaper.

Over the past several years further restoration work has been completed, including the construction of a new cupola to replace the one which once graced this picturesque building more than half a century ago.

Victoria Harbour Lumber Company, general store and public library.

The Telephone Exchange

LONG AGO IN our grandmother's house, an old-fashioned crank-style telephone hung on the wall opposite the china cabinet. This telephone facinated me to no end. Raised in the city, as I was, it amazed me that Grandma didn't have a "real" phone, the same as we did. I often cranked it up just to hear the lady say, "Number please," and then immediately replaced the earpiece before anyone caught me playing with it.

It was nearly eighty-nine years ago that the first telephone exchange was set up in the village. In 1910 a switchboard was located in the offices of Victoria Harbour Lumber Company. It was later moved to the rear of Archie Thorburn's tailor shop, where Miss Pearl Crooke became the first telephone operator. There were less than half a dozen phones in the village then, but as the number of subscribers increased, Pansy Fox, who worked in the tailor shop, was hired to assist Miss Crooke. Several years later the exchange was relocated in the Masonic Temple building.

Gordon Alliston was the first manager and was instrumental in the formation of the new telephone system. For many years the service was only available between 8 a.m. and 9 p.m. After service was extended to twenty-four hours a day, Mr. Alliston handled the night calls.

In 1926 Miss Ena Lidstone became an operator, a position she would hold for more than four decades.

By 1929 a committee had been formed from among members of the town council and in that year William Grigg became the new manager.

The Tay Telephone System made its last move, to a new building alongside the old office, in 1959. On Sunday, December 15, 1968, at 2:10 a.m., villagers made the change from the old crank wall telephones to the new dial system, ending another golden era—although it seems few regretted it.

Victoria Harbour residents celebrate the end of World War I with a Victory Parade along William Street. Here grades five and eight are passing by Reid's general store. Note both the Union Jack and the Stars and Stripes (centre of store).
—COURTESY MRS. EPLETT

The War Years

THEY CALLED IT the "war to end all wars." In cities and towns and villages across the country, railway stations were full of new recruits, red, white and blue bunting and Union Jacks were draped everywhere. Cheering crowds lined the platforms and filled the streets, weeping women waving lace-edged hankies blew kisses, threw flowers, made promises and prayed, while military bands, church bands and club bands played on. Middle-aged sergeants and lieutenants, their broad chests ablaze with stripes and medals, marched away thousands of fresh-faced, eager young recruits. Many of the young men considered it a first-rate lark, the ideal opportunity for a lad to show what he was made of. But others knew better.

Years later the same scene would be re-enacted as more young men and women left home to serve in yet another war. For those who returned, it was a jubilant time, with cheering crowds and bands and parades in their honour. Those who never came back found their final resting places on foreign soil, thousands of miles from their homes, families and friends.

In Victoria Harbour commemorative plaques grace the walls of the churches. In St. Paul's Presbyterian Church one was erected in memory of Lt. C. Percival Waldie, killed in action; Walter Scott Waldie, who died at Phyl Military Camp in Wales; and Gunner John Albert Scott, who died at Orpington Hospital in England. Twenty-eight church members fought, including two nursing sisters, Lieutenants Edyth E. Herron Scott and Joan F. Scott.

Victoria Harbour, like thousands of other towns and villages across the country, suffered its share of losses among its residents. On Albert Street stands a cenotaph commemorating their sons and daughters who fought during World War I and World War II.

> France,
> October 5th, 1918.
> My dear Mrs. Clark :
> May I write you a few lines in regard to your boy, who was recently killed in action here in France. I know how eager you as his mother must be, to have any news whatever regarding his death. He was a boy of real promise, and his name had gone in for a commission, in the Flying Corps, I believe.
> He left his battery headquarters one evening, and in going forward to a new position, he evidently became separated from his comrades and came under shell fire along a main road. It was then he was killed. He was buried by one of our Canadian chaplains in a cemetery called "Ontario Cemetery" and he lies among fellow Canadians. I went over yesterday and found his grave, marked by a small cross, with his name, number, battery and date of death marked on it. He was killed Friday morning, Sept. 27th probably, or there is a chance that it was during the preceding evening, the 26th.
> May God comfort you. I can only try to imagine what your sorrow is. May you find peace and joy in the knowledge that you gave one of the very best to a great cause and that your boy died nobly as he had lived

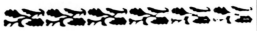

The Monsters of Georgian Bay

BACK IN THE late 1800s and early 1900s commercial fisheries thrived on Georgian Bay. Sturgeon, whitefish, muskellunge, bass and lake trout were caught off the shores of Victoria Harbour. One of the early fish plants in town was owned by Mr. Booth. Booth operated his fish house where Mackenzie Park now stands on the shores of Georgian Bay.

Monstrous sturgeon, some as long as seven feet and weighing over a hundred and seventy-five pounds, were caught in the waters of Georgian Bay by using large nets. By 1910 Booth's fish plant was shipping boxcar loads of these huge sturgeon, packed in ice, to New York City, where caviar—made from the roe—was a delicacy favoured by the rich.

Mr. Booth continued to operate the fish company until the early 1920s, when Charlie Malcolm bought the fish house. Malcolm continued to haul in large fish, which he shipped to ready markets across the country. Village resident Florence Belcher remembers a day when Malcolm himself caught a sturgeon so large that he was able to sell it and buy a suit of clothes, a gallon of whiskey, and a cow with the profits.

The Anderson Fish Company was only one of the many fisheries once located in Victoria Harbour. Photo c.1900.
—COURTESY MRS. EPLETT

Examples of the monster sturgeon once caught in Hogg's Bay. Ham Vent is on the left, Joe Heels on the right, but who's the lad in the middle? Photo c.1900.
—COURTESY MRS. EPLETT

A Bridge Through Time

THE TRANQUILITY OF the summer's afternoon was broken only by the shrieking whistle of the steam locomotive as it clattered down the track. The grey-black smoke billowing from its single smokestack lingered in the air long after the train had passed. The sound of the chugging engines and the distant smell of smoke was common to the residents of Victoria Harbour, particularly to those who lived near the Hogg's Bay trestle.

Built in the winter of 1907-8 it stretched over the swampy waters of Hogg Bay from Victoria Harbour to the newly constructed C.P.R. grain elevators on Maple Island, later to be filled in and renamed Port McNicoll, in honour of D. McNicoll, vice-president of C.P.R. The trestle was designed and built for the Canadian Pacific Railway by Mike McPeake, a local builder. McPeake used only the finest B.C. fir and pine timbers available for this great undertaking. When the structure was finally completed, it was 2,141 feet long and fifty feet high, thus having the distinction of being the longest wooden trestle in the Dominion.

The purpose of the trestle was to connect the mainland with Maple Island, where the new terminal and freight yards were built. Also built were two freight sheds and the town's railroad station on the north side of the slip. C.P.R. owned and operated five passenger steamships, the *Assiniboia, Keewatin, Manitoba, Alberta* and the *Athabasca*. The railway also ran what were called boat trains from Toronto to Port McNicoll, where the passengers would connect with one of the ships to enjoy a week's cruise on the lakes. This service was finally discontinued in 1966.

In 1956 steam power was replaced by diesel power. A common practice was to have one man walk over the trestle in front of the train to watch for dangerous stress caused by the 518,000-pound diesels. Although only one derailment ever occurred on the structure, in 1971 C.P.R. found it unfit and unsafe to support the heavier trains.

For over six years the wooden landmark sat unused. After several attempts to save it from the wrecking ball and have it preserved as an historic site, the trestle was finally torn down and sold for scrap in the winter of 1977-78.

On October 18, 1981, an historic plaque was unveiled near the site of the trestle to commemorate the structure.

A nostalgic moment as the last steam engine passes over the Hogg's Bay trestle on April 30, 1960.
—COURTESY CHARLES HEELS

"The Hole in the Wall"—all that remains of the old trestle underpass at Victoria Harbour.

Maple Island, Victoria Harbor, Ont.

Construction of the C.P.R. grain elevator on Maple Island (Port McNicoll) c.1909.   —COURTESY STANLEY BOYER

Many village residents were employed at the grain elevators. This photo c.1920s. Among the men pictured here are Dorsey St. Amant, Charlie Latondresse, David Moore, Joseph Hull, Paddy Kelly, Mr. Cadeau, Ernie Cadeau, Ernie Dupuis and Charlie Schissler.
—COURTESY CLARENCE SYKES

The Victoria Harbour Ferry Service. In the early days, two well-known vessels, the Alda and the Breeze, operated between Victoria Harbour and Port McNicoll transporting workers to and from the grain elevator. Later, John Gilmore offered the same service until 1943 with his ferry, the Kayak. c.1930.
—COURTESY MRS. M. JARMAN

"Lots of notes in the oats!" During the First World War the girls at the grain elevators in Port McNicoll kept in touch with our boys "over there" by stuffing notes in grain bags heading overseas.
—COURTESY OF CLARENCE SYKES

Gordon Gervais, Chief Engineer on the Keewatin.
—COURTESY MRS. M. GERVAIS

The Keewatin *docked at Port McNicoll c.1930s.*
—COURTESY STANLEY BOYER

The Queen's Hotel on Richard Street dates back to the 1870s. For many years the Queen's was the only "wet spot" in town. It was partially destroyed by fire nearly half a century ago. Today its main floor serves as a private residence. —COURTESY MRS. EPLETT

Richard Street, Victoria Harbor, Ont.

The Queen's Hotel

RECORDS INDICATE THAT the Queen's Hotel may have been built as early as 1870. The land on which it stands today was first owned by the Northern Mercantile Company. Whether or not the existing brick structure is the same building built by the N.M.C. is uncertain. It may well have been a frame hotel. We do know that William Casselman was the proprietor in 1872.

In 1900 the property was sold to Isabella Harrel, and according to the Farmer's and Business Directory in 1901, Daniel Robbins became the next owner. The Queen's was the only hotel in the village until 1902, when the Victoria Harbour Lumber Company built the Royal Victoria on Albert Street.

The Royal Victoria catered mainly to out-of-town lumber agents, business executives and tourists. It also played host to various village functions and ladies' groups. The Royal neither sold nor allowed intoxicating spirits on its premises.

The Queen's Hotel, however, did sell liquor and had the only taproom for miles around. Their clientele consisted largely of travelling salesmen, millworkers and tourists. A shot of whiskey sold for twenty-five cents, cigars and newspapers could be purchased from the newsstand in the lobby. At the turn of the century the Queen's dining room was said to be one of the best, where a decent meal could be had for under a dollar.

Because the Queen's was the only "wet" spot in town, it eventually acquired a reputation for being a disreputable place, where drunks could often be found sprawled out in the street on Sunday mornings, much to the horror of the village ladies.

Today the old hotel on Richard Street is barely recognizable minus its mansard roof, its two upper storeys and its verandah. The ground floor was salvaged from a fire that nearly destroyed it in 1920. It survives today as a private residence.

Wanted.

Good, strong girl, accustomed to hotel work. Good wages and good home. Apply to

Mrs J. J. Robins,
The Queen's Hotel.

Early employees of the company store pose in this rare 1905 photograph.　　　　　　—COURTESY LACAC

The Company Store

IN 1902, THE same year that the company office and the hotel were built, another building was being scheduled for construction—the company store. The new store was another boon to the village, especially the workers in the mill. Typical of most general stores of that era in both size and the vast array of goods it stocked, the company store soon became a favourite gathering place, with local gossip traded over the counter along with the week's grocery order.

Its wood-finished interior was lit by gaslight and heated by wood. Its long wooden counters and floor-to-ceiling shelves spilled over with colourful bolts of sprigged cotton and gingham. Enamel cookware and kitchen china vied for space alongside oil lamps, chewing tobacco and canned goods. The aisles were crowded with bushel baskets, galvanized tubs and ready-to-wear clothes. Coils of rope and various tools hung from nails. There was everything from soup to nuts. If the company store didn't have it, chances were that no one else did either.

Mill employees' wages were paid in part with "script vouchers" that could only be used in the store. Change owing from cash purchases was returned by means of a trolley conveyer sent down to the clerk from the office on the second floor. In times of distress, such as illness or layoffs, credit was issued to the family. The phrase "I owe my soul to the company store" was in some cases very true.

The store was managed by R. J. Neilly, with both male and female clerks. In 1903 John Waldie

sold the store to the Victoria Harbour Mercantile Company, who operated it until the mills closed down in 1927. That year it was purchased by John Petroff, who operated an automobile repair shop on the premises for seven years. The next owner was Mr. R. Evans, who in turn sold it in 1944 to Bruce Eplett. The Epletts had a hardware store and a garage with gas pumps out front. In the late 1940s the entire building was turned into a hardware store and the garage and pumps removed. Around this same time, the old company store received a drastic facelift. Modernization included the removal of all the fancy gingerbread trim from the top of the building, the removal of the front windows, and covering of the entire structure with aluminum siding.

Sharon and Clinton Todd became the next owners in 1979 and renamed the store Harbour Hardware Limited. Later the Todds, in co-operation with the village Local Architectural Conservation Advisory Committee (LACAC) and with help from the Ministry of Citizenship and Culture, set out to completely restore this grand old general store, now recognized as an historical structure.

After considerable research, work was begun with the help of local craftspeople. Parts of the building were reconstructed with materials from another old building in Vasey dating back to the same period. Extensive foundation work was done to strengthen the building, as well as new support beams, a new roof and further duplication of any original gingerbread trim if repair was not possible. The last step in the total restoration of the company store was the application of the final coat of canary yellow paint.

Old-timers remarked on that day that it was like stepping back in time to see the old store looking as it did back in 1902, when it first opened its doors. It remains today a wonderful example of an old-time general store, a visible reminder of the days when the Harbour was a thriving mill town.

Eplett's Hardware c.1940s.   —COURTESY MRS. EPLETT

Village Churches

THE VILLAGE CHURCH stands today as a testament to the faith of our pioneering forefathers and was often the first public building to be erected in most early Ontario settlements. The church played an integral part in the lives of the villagers. It was the scene of social gatherings, town meetings, annual bazaars, card parties, Saturday-night dances and potluck suppers. The church was also a sanctuary for prayer and a haven for its parishioners.

The Church of St. Joseph was the first church in Huronia and was built by the French Jesuit fathers at Fort Ste. Marie, between Victoria Harbour and Midland. After the arrival of the first settlers the Methodist circuit rider, or saddlebag preacher, as they were most often called, soon became a familiar sight along the rutted dirt roads throughout Ontario. Before long other denominations followed suit, establishing their churches in settled areas.

The first three churches in Victoria Harbour were the Anglican Church, built in the mid-1870s by the Church of England. Across the road stood the little clapboard Methodist Church, where St. John's United Church stands today. The third church was a Roman Catholic Mission Church built in 1874. Traces of all three churches have long since vanished.

St. Paul's Presbyterian Church - 1906

Perhaps one of the last legacies left to the village by John Waldie was his gift of a church. Perched on a hill overlooking the bay stands St. Paul's Presbyterian Church. Unique in its architecture, the white clapboard structure is said to closely resemble a church near Mr. Waldie's birthplace in Scotland. The church site was originally owned by William Ardagh. In 1876 it became the property of Richard Power, who in turn sold it to the Victoria Harbour Lumber Company in 1889.

The Presbyterian congregation was made up largely of lumber company executives, mill foremen and their families. Prior to the building of the new church, the people shared facilities with the Methodists, with their own ministers officiating at alternate services in the little frame church on William Street.

Construction began in 1905 and the building was ready for its dedication and opening ceremonies by June 24, 1906.

Two years earlier the Women's Foreign Missionary Society was formed, as well as the Victoria Mission Band, led by the wife of Rev. J. R. Burnett. By 1909 the first official Sunday School was formed by Mr. John Edgar, with an enrolment of over one hundred. That same year the first church choir was organized, led by J. Wilson, with Miss Emma Smyth as organist. The Ladies Aid came into being on March 11, 1909, and the ladies made themselves responsible for the care of the church and manse. In 1914 the Women's Foreign Mission was amalgamated with the Women's Home Missionary Society.

Over the past eighty-two years more than

a dozen home ministers have preached from the pulpit. Among them were the Rev. J. R. Burnett (1904-1908) and the Rev. H. A. Berlis (1909-1912).

On Sunday, June 24, 1956, the congregation celebrated the church's fiftieth anniversary, with their pastor Rev. Charles Carter and guest speaker Rev. R. J. Berlis of Montreal, son of a former minister.

Down through the years the membership roll included the names of many old village families, many of whose descendants still reside in Victoria Harbour today: the Gills, the E. Crookes, Lumsden, Duckworth, McKinnons, H. J. Schissler, J. E. Smyth, Gilmour, McNab, Scott, T. Brown, Houston, Gardiner, Ball, Wm. Morres, the Stoddards, the Belfrys, the Bells, and the Thorburns.

Today the old church remains much as it did all those years ago, though its white picket fence has vanished and the trees have matured with time.

St. Paul's Presbyterian Church, built in 1906 by John Waldie, president of the Victoria Harbour Lumber Company.

The Early History of St. John's - 1895

On the site of the Church Hall there once stood a little Methodist Church just behind where the present-day United Church stands. The earliest available records show that one time Victoria Harbour, Midland and Ebenezer were all part of the Penetanguishene Circuit (1882), with the Reverend R. Strachan officiating services at these three locations.

On August 15, 1887, Victoria Harbour and Ebenezer became part of the Wyevale Methodist Circuit and services were held alternately at the two churches.

For many years the Methodist congregation shared facilities with their Presbyterian neighbours, who called themselves a Union Church, and for a while student ministers of both denominations held alternate services morning and evening at the little church.

In 1895 it was decided that a new church building was needed and two local carpenters, Mr. Sam Burns and his son Chris, were contracted to build it. The following year a fine new wood-framed church was erected on the site of the original building and was surrounded by a neat white picket fence. In 1906 the Presbyterian congregation moved to their new home church on Ellen Street.

Women have always played an integral part in church life and at St. John's it was no different. The first Ladies Aid was established in 1900 and a flurry of activity soon began. Garden parties, strawberry socials, afternoon teas and bazaars, as well as catering at the Masonic Lodge meetings and serving

St. John's United Church, Victoria Harbour.

lunch at Waldie's Rink, became part of their program. They also arranged social suppers and annual moonlight excursions on the S.S. *John Lee*, which became the highlight of the season over the years.

In 1919 an auxiliary of the W.M.S. was formed, and in 1933 they amalgamated to form the Women's Association, which twenty-nine years later became known as the United Church Women.

During those earlier years church members were actively involved in both the Junior and Senior League, the Mission Band, the Young People's Society, and the Brean Bible Classes.

In 1925 the congregation joined the Church Union to become part of the United Church of Canada. Since 1882 more than forty ministers and students have officiated at services held at St. John's. The Reid family, the Burns, the Taylors, Vaseys, Epletts, Campbells and the Vents are only a few of the old names which date back to those earlier days in St. John's Church history.

Burns family.   —COURTESY VERA BOYER

Vent family.

St. Mary's Church - 1882-1937; 1937-

On October 19, 1882, the Roman Catholic Episcopal Corporation purchased lots six and seven on the south side of William Street from Ellen and Richard Power of Victoria Harbour. Because of its large Roman Catholic population, a rather big church house was required. In 1883 the new bell housed in the graceful belvedere rang for the first time. The church was of a typical design for that era, batten on board with tall, gothic arched windows surrounding it. The building was heated by wood and lit by gaslight. Its interior was pine.

For more than half a century the church bell rang out through the village every Sunday morning calling its congregation to worship. There are those who remember the old bell tolling on Armistice Day in 1918 and those who recall the last Sunday the church bell rang. On April 13, 1937, at approximately 7:30 p.m., a fire broke out in the home of church caretaker Hector St. Amant and quickly spread to the neighbouring church. Within two hours nothing remained of St. Mary's except charred, smouldering ruins. It was a sad night as villagers gathered around with their pastor, Father McNamara, who gave thanks

that no one was hurt in the blaze.

For the remainder of the spring and all that summer Catholics attended church at St. Paul's, alternating services with their Presbyterian neighbours. That autumn a new St. Mary's Church was built on the hill above William Street, on the west side of Albert. The building was erected by many willing hands, a small clapboard structure with a flat-top tower.

St. Mary's like the other two churches in the village, played an important part in the lives of its people. Some of the early pastors were Father Bernard Doyle (1919-1929). Father D. W. McNamara (1929-1941), Father J. G. Loftus (1941) and Father Wm. A. Kennedy (mid-1940s).

St. Mary's Roman Catholic Cemetery

On a clear, crisp autumn day, from the top of the hill you can see far out into the bay. The old cemetery where many of our pioneering families lie is situated on the west half of lot 14, concession 8, and comprises 4.06 acres of land. On 13 November 1920 this property was transferred to the Roman Catholic Episcopal for the sum of one dollar by David Robbins of Victoria Harbour.

The names are mostly French (Arbour, Juneau, Boyer, Ladouceur, Moreau, Cadeau, Cousineau, Bergie, and Pelletier) with a number of Irish (O'Shea, O'Brien, McVoy, McBrien, and Wilson), all connected in one way or another with the history of the village and the mills that built it.

St. Mary's Catholic Church, built in 1937 after the big fire.

This rare photo was taken in the early 1880s. The log structure may have been S.S. No. 10. — COURTESY THEO BERNARD

The Red Brick Schoolhouse

THE FIRST SCHOOLHOUSE in the village was located on the southeast corner of Albert and Richard streets. The one-room frame school was erected in the late 1870s and known locally as the Evergreen School. Early records indicate that in 1880 Charles Shott, a native of Ireland, was the schoolteacher. In 1902 a new school was built on the north side of William Street across from the lighthouse. Thereafter the old Evergreen School served many different purposes before it was eventually destroyed by fire.

Although the new school was much larger than its predecessor it had only two rooms. It was built on a fieldstone foundation and set well back from the road. The building's batten-board exterior sported sixteen gothic arched windows and two entrances. Its interior featured high ceilings, pine floors and wainscotting throughout.

By 1906 it was apparent that another school was required due to the increasing population of the village. The board of trustees approved the construction of a modern two-storey brick schoolhouse to be built directly in front of the existing one.

The following year the new Victoria Harbour Public School was officially opened with the tolling of the new school bell. The design was typical of that era with a three-storey square tower housing the main entrance. Inside, a graceful double oak staircase led the way to the classrooms on the top floor. Crowning the tower was a cupola where the bell was located. For more than half a century the sound of the bell was as much a part of village history as the pealing of church bells on Sunday mornings.

Around the turn of the century a teacher who graduated from Normal School (Teacher's College) could receive an annual salary of up to $800. Teachers were expected to act as both nurse and babysitter as well as provide the basic rudiments of an education. In those early days teachers taught from *The Canadian Teacher* and *The Home and School*. Some will remember the "Mary, John and Peter" reader, the *Ontario Reader,* the *Ontario Public School Composition and Grammar* books and the *Canadian Speller.*

The School was divided into five classrooms. Grades two and three used the ground floor room facing the road; grades four and five were in the room behind it. On the upper floor were grades six and seven in the back room and grade eight, which the principal taught, in the classroom facing the street. Grade one occupied an old classroom in the original batten-board school. The other room was used as a lunch room and library. Behind the school were the "privies"—six-holers.

During the winter months those boys who lived near Vent's Farm often skated to school and back by way of Hogg's River and the bay.

As do children everywhere those from the Harbour played the usual pranks on their teachers. Some older residents might recall an incident when one teacher was locked in the privy for a considerable length of time while boys ran around the perimeter banging on the walls. Finally the principal came to the rescue of the embarrassed teacher who had been caught with his drawers down. Other mischief included cutting the rope for the school bell or placing mice or frogs in the teacher's desk. Those unfortunate enough to be caught became the recipients of the dreaded strap that hung ominously by the teacher's door.

One of the best-remembered principals was Clarence Moore, who taught from the late thirties until the early sixties. Back in his early days as school principal, Clarence was given the nickname of "Peanut Moore" by his students, a name which stuck for many years. According to the story, there was a train that ran round trip daily from Orillia to Midland, called the peanut train. Twice a day it passed by the school blowing its obnoxious whistle, much to the distress of Mr. Moore who claimed it distracted his class. His verbal complaints soon earned him the title "Peanut Moore."

In the days of prohibition, it was not

Grades 3, 4 and 5 photographed outside the old school-house on William Street c.1903.
—COURTESY MRS. EPLETT

unusual for some families to make their own supply of moonshine. Around that time three young village lads devised a plan to acquire a few bottles of brew without being caught. One night the boys, Andy, Ernest and Isadore, waited patiently for darkness to fall. Isadore's father kept his stock in an upstairs bedroom so, it seemed simple enough for Isidore to lower the quart bottles down on a rope from the window to his pals below. They would untie the bottles with care, give a tug on the rope and repeat the process until they had enough. Things went well until the unexpected arrival of Isadore's father, who sent them running for home, took the boys' place. Isadore, unaware of what was happening, continued to lower the bottles down to his

Victoria Harbour Public School.

father, who hauled them through the pantry window directly below his son. No one knows for certain what happened to Isadore but to this day, the story always brings a hearty laugh from a certain gentleman who was there on that night nearly fifty years ago.

Former students fondly recall skating parties out on the bay, games of shinny in the schoolyard and Arbour Day, when everyone trouped across Hopkin's farm to plant trees. At Christmas the classrooms were decorated and a large evergreen was cut down by some of the older boys and lavishly trimmed by the girls. There was an annual Christmas concert held at the Orange Hall, where everyone received candy, an orange and one small gift.

Some of the early teachers and principals were John Gillespie, Mr. Fallis, Clarence Moore, Miss Bessie Winfield (who at one time taught all the grades in the original school), Marjory J. Mount (who retired in 1969 and who also taught in the old building), Miss Chisholm, Miss Frances MacKenzie, Miss Murphey, Marjory Vent, Elizabeth N. Sitter, Violet Lidstone and Mary Germain.

In 1952 a Catholic school was built in the village to accommodate the large number of Catholic students. St. Mary's was officially opened in the autumn of 1952 with Father Howe, Sister Mary Carmel and the entire church congregation present. Sister St. Thaddeus and Sister St. Monica, respectively, followed Sister Mary as principal. Some of the first teachers were Miss A. Savue, Sister M. Regina, H. Dubois and N. Giroux.

Nine years later a new public school was built on MacKenzie Street. In 1967 an addition was added to the building.

Today the old red brick schoolhouse stands abandoned on a weed-choked lot. Its windows are cracked and caked with years of dirt and grime, and some of the doors hang drunkenly on rusty old hinges. The bell and cupola have long since been removed, as has the tunnel fire escape and the picket fence which once flanked the schoolyard along William Street. Inside, little is left of the original classrooms or the oak staircase and landings that thundered, with the pounding of a thousand small feet. Filth and debris and old machinery parts litter the scarred floorboards. Interior walls have been removed—evidence that at some time the building served another purpose.

However, in the grade one classroom in the original part of the school, time appears to have stood still as brilliant streams of April sunshine pour through tall arched windows and memories linger in the air. Despite the rubble and chaos of fallen plaster and strapping that litter the room, one can almost be transported back to the turn of the century, when rows of carved desktops bore proof that another generation was proficient in the art of jackknife. On the wall above the blackboard a portrait of the reigning monarch, flanked by Union Jacks, and on the surrounding walls the alphabet in capitals and small letters on cardboard squares. At the rear of the room are neat rows of small hooks where thousands of caps and coats have hung.

One wonders if the old red brick schoolhouse will be standing for our grandchildren to see or if, like so many other buildings of significance, it will be doomed because of lack of interest or money to restore this fine old structure.

—COURTESY MICHAEL BOYER

Any fire in the village was cause for concern. Note the hand-drawn hose reel. Is that someone leaning out the window in the house on the right? c.1900.
—COURTESY LACAC

Village Fires

BACK IN THE early days, fire was a major concern and a threat to the village of Victoria Harbour, its buildings constructed almost entirely of wood. There have been four major blazes in the past hundred years.

In the 1890s the Victoria Harbour Lumber Company started their own fire brigade, complete with buckets, hoses and a steam pump. They watched over the mills and downtown section. On March 27, 1902, the first of the four major fires rocked the small village. At about 9:30 a.m. a small fire began in the basement of the two-year-old company boarding house. The blaze quickly raged through the large wood-framed structure and went on to ignite the newly constructed company offices across the road. The Midland fire brigade was called in but arrived too late to save the boarding house, company offices, Thorburn's Tailor Shop, and another store, but with the help of the V.H.L.C. fire brigade and village residents, Gardiner's Studio Gallery was saved. The estimated loss to the V.H.L.C. was between $40,000 and $50,000.

That same year the boarding house was rebuilt and renamed the Royal Victoria Hotel. In 1961 the old hotel burned to the ground. The company offices were rebuilt in 1902. They were also destroyed by fire, in 1958.

Ten years later the second blaze lit the skies of Victoria Harbour. In 1912 an explosion occurred in the basement of Rumball's Hardware Store on Albert Street. Clarence Sykes, a long-time resident of Victoria Harbour, remembers that day.

He had just purchased a gallon of kerosene and was riding away on his bicycle when the front windows blew out. Fire spread quickly through the store and adjoining buildings. By day's end Rumball's Hardware Store, Burnie's Jewellery Store, T. Brown's Drugstore, the Toronto Bank, the Gem Theatre, and apartments were destroyed by the fire. The Toronto Bank building still exists today, but only the main floor remains.

On July 9, 1932, a spectacular early morning fire levelled the main business block of the village. At about 8 a.m. a fire broke out in the storeroom to the rear of Philip Moreau's General Store on William Street. Across the road, mechanic John Jackson had just fuelled a car at the Victoria Garage (the old company store) when he noticed smoke pouring from between the Bank of Commerce building and Moreau's store. Within minutes an alarm was issued. The fire was still in its early stages when an attempt was made to extinguish it. Several men tried in vain to quell the blaze with the aid of a garden hose, which proved useless. In the meantime the Midland Fire Brigade was called. They arrived within seventeen minutes. By this time the area was crowded with onlookers and everyone was frantic. The town was without fire hydrants and the fire hose proved too short to reach the bay. A temporary pier was built to enable the truck to back over the sand to reach the water.

During all this the flames were fanned by a

brisk wind, quickly igniting the roof of the bank, while manager Mr. Harrington, with the aid of several men, managed to rescue all the bank's records. Meanwhile Douglas Robertson, whose photography studio was above the bank, and Miss Annie Carly, whose apartment was located over the store, both managed to save most of their furniture with the help of a dozen men who ran between the burning structures and the

William Street facing east. Everyone gathers at the scene of the big blaze of 1912. —COURTESY MRS. EPLETT

garage where everything was deposited.

By now the fire brigade had enough water pressure, but the heat was so intense that two plate-glass windows blew out. Across the street, on the southeast corner, men soaked down the fronts of the old Bank of Toronto building, Lorne Ball's drugstore and Roy Heel's groceteria. Flying sparks ignited other fires on the roofs of nearby houses, but these were quickly extinguished by men using buckets.

By 12:30 the buildings on the southwest corner lay in smouldering ruins. A mere hundred and twenty-five feet away, on south Albert, a shell of four standing walls was all that remained of the Oddfellows' Temple, its roof and interior badly gutted. Douglas Robertson lost all his photographic equipment. His insurance policy had expired only two weeks earlier. Hurt and bewidered, he and his family stood with others contemplating their losses and thanking God for

The 1912 fire destroyed five businesses including the Bank of Toronto pictured here. At the far left is the Gem Theatre.
—COURTESY MRS. EPLETT

their lives.

Five years later, on April 13, 1937, the fourth big blaze hit the town. At approximately 7:30 p.m. a fire broke out in the kitchen of Hector St. Amant's home and quickly spread in both directions. Help was summoned immediately and the village volunteer fire brigade worked relentlessly to prevent the flames from further destruction until the arrival of more help and equipment from both the Midland and Coldwater fire departments. Water was pumped up from the bay through more than 2,300 feet of hose.

Within a space of two hours, four houses and St. Mary's Catholic Church were totally engulfed by flames that lit up the whole village. By midnight nothing remained, only wet, smouldering ruins.

In 1950 the village purchased their first fire truck, a 1919 LaFrance, from the Toronto Fire Department. It was one of the many trucks used in fighting the famous *Noronic* fire in Toronto's harbour, a fire which tragically killed 112 passengers in 1949. Storage of the brigade's fire fighting equipment was difficult at the best of times. Before purchasing the LaFrance the brigade stored their auxiliary pump and big hose reel in Moore's garage, behind his hardware store at Albert and Richard streets, where the cenotaph now stands.

It wasn't until 1951 that the brigade moved into their new firehall on Albert Street. In 1956 the fire brigade was incorporated as a volunteer fire department, with twenty men and Don (Did) Cadeau as fire chief.

In 1962 the village bought their second fire truck, from the Hamilton Fire Department. One year later, in 1963, the old LaFrance was sold to the Penetang High School where it was to be used in parades and at high school football games.

In 1980 the LaFrance was sold to a collector in Midland, Ontario, where it remains today as a relic of early firefighting in Ontario.

1950 Volunteer Firemen

CHIEF	—William J. Reid
CAPTAIN	—William E. Quinlan
LIEUTENANT	—Gilbert Brodeur
ENGINEERS	—Bruce Crooke, Clarence Sykes, Wilbert Moreau
HOSEMEN	—Wilfred Savage, Bruce Eplett, Walter Lumsden
NOZZLEMEN	—Lorne Ball, Fred Miller, Lawrence Arbour

The village's first fire truck — a 1919 LaFrance.

—COURTESY VICTORIA HARBOUR VOLUNTEER FIRE DEPT.

Cliff Moore's Esso station on old Highway 12 (Park Street). Note the old Orange Kist clock. After 36 years it still keeps perfect time.
—COURTESY JEAN MOORE

Early Gas Stations

FILL-ER-UP PLEASE! That familiar phrase has been heard throughout the village since the late 1920s, when two of the oldest remaining businesses opened their doors for the first time.

Who can forget the days of the Ford model A, rumble seats, hand-pumped gas, free travel maps, and catchy slogans like Texaco's "You can trust your car to the man who wears the star," or Esso's "Put a tiger in your tank"?

Moore's Esso

In the summer of 1927 Robert J. Moore, his wife, Lizzie, and family moved from their modest log cabin on Sturgeon Bay to their new home in Victoria Harbour, where Robert started a silver fox farm. Two years later, in 1929, he built a small shack in front of their home and opened the town's first Esso gas station. In the beginning they offered only gasoline, coal oil and cigarettes, but later included bread and dry goods as well.

Robert continued to operate the business with the help of his wife until 1947, when his youngest son, Clifford, took over the family business. Cliff, who had always been in the retail business, sold his own general store in Phelpson and moved back to Victoria Harbour. By the 1950s, with the help of his wife, Jean, Cliff Moore was offering everything from motor oil to cooking oil.

The year 1956 was a tragic one for the Moore family. On September 2, Lizzie McKenzie died, and not quite two months later, on October 27, Robert J. Moore died.

In 1969 Moore's Esso was given a service award from Imperial Oil in recognition of forty years of continuous service—the plaque still hangs proudly on the wall of the office. In 1980 Cliff celebrated forty years in the retail business, thirty-three of that in

Robert Moore and his old hound dog sniff out prey c.1940s.
—COURTESY JEAN MOORE

Victoria Harbour, making him the senior merchant of the village. In that same year, Cliff's youngest son, Dwaine, followed in his father's footsteps and took over the family business. On October 18, 1986, after a long illness, Clifford Moore passed on.

Today Moore's Esso still offers the same friendly atmosphere Robert J. offered sixty years ago.

Petroff's Service Station

Born in Bulgaria, John Petroff immigrated to Canada in 1914 with his wife, Vivien. They first settled in Port Severn, where John found employment at the Port Severn locks. In the early 1920s John and Vivien moved to Kay Corners to open their first garage.

In 1927 John purchased the old company store at William and Albert streets, and converted the store into garages and a new car showroom. John also installed gas pumps on the sidewalk, where he pumped gas for the McCall Frontenac Oil Co. and later for Imperial Oil. John and Vivien lived above the showroom for seven years before building a new service station and house beside the Union Cemetery on Park Street in 1934

For the next twenty-one years John operated under the City Service banner, until 1955, when his son Lorne took over the family business. Today Lorne operates the business as a Shell station and continues to offer the same friendly service his father, John Petroff, offered sixty-one years ago.

John Petroff's tow truck, 1937. —COURTESY LORNE PETROFF

John Petroff's garage in the old company store, 1930.

William St., Looking North, Victoria Harbor, Ont.

The intersection of William and Albert streets. Contrary to what it says on the photograph, the camera looks east onto William Street. On the right are the Bank of Toronto and a bakery, and across the road are millworkers' cottages, each one surrounded by a whitewashed picket fence. This photo c. 1890. —COURTESY MRS. EPLETT

94

Victoria Harbour Properties

PROPERTY	BUILT	HISTORY
Mill No. 1	1869	torn down, rebuilt 1890s
Mill No. 2	1869	destroyed by fire 1918, rebuilt 1919, dismantled 1927
Mill No. 3	1900	parts removed, the rest demolished 1927
The Company Store	1902	still exists
The Company Office	1902	destroyed by fire, rebuilt same year, burned 1957
The Company Boarding House	1890s	burned in 1902, hotel and boarding house rebuilt same year, destroyed by fire in 1961
First Railway Station	1879	torn down 1890s
Second Railway Station	1890s	torn down late 1960s
St. Mary's R. C. Church	1874	burned 1937
Second St. Mary's Church	1938	still exists
The Church of England	1870s	burned 1880s
St. Paul's Presbyterian Church	1907	still exists
St. John's United Church	1895	still exists
Methodist Church	1882	torn down 1895
The Standard Bank	—	burned 1932

PROPERTY	BUILT	HISTORY
Douglas Robertson Photography Studio	—	burned 1932
Oddfellows Temple	—	gutted by fire 1932
Harbour Cafe and Ice Cream Parlour	—	burned 1932
New Era Newspaper	1914	out of business 1919
The Queen's Hotel	—	partially destroyed by fire 1920
Rumball's Hardware Store	—	burned 1912
Jim Burnie's Jewellery Store	—	burned 1912
Drug Store	—	burned 1912
Allison's Undertaking	—	burned in 1918
Gem Theatre	1910	burned 1912
Crystal Theatre	1912	burned 1918
Millinery Shop	—	burned 1918
Library	1916	still exists
The Waldie Ice Rink	1905	burned in 1922
Reid's General Store	1895	closed in 1961
Evergreen School	1880	destroyed by fire
The Red Brick School	1907	still standing
Moore's Esso	1929	still exists
Masonic Hall	1917	still exists
Petroff's Service Station	1934	now Shell station

GEM THEATRE
VICTORIA HARBOR

MONDAY and TUESDAY NIGHTS

"Boy Scouts"

Wednesday and Thursday, June 11th and 12th,

"$5000 REWARD

For Information Leading to the Capture of
DICK ARLINGTON"

FRIDAY and SATURDAY NIGHTS

"THE BRASS BULLET"

Admission 15 and 10 Cents.

CORNER BUSINESS SECTION. VICTORIA HARBOR, ONT.

—COURTESY MRS. EPLETT

The Masonic Temple was built in 1914.
—COURTESY MICHAEL BOYER

Best friends Clarence Sykes, Lionel and Raymond Asselin pose on the sidewalk outside the old company store in the 1940s.
—COURTESY CLARENCE SYKES

Wedding Day photo of Mr. and Mrs. Bruce Eplett. —COURTESY MRS. EPLETT

List of Freehold Residents 1880

NAME	CONCESSION	LOT	NAME	CONCESSION	LOT
Arthurs, Stephen	7	14	McIndoo, Jas.	6	8
Atkinson, John	5	12	McLeod, John	S	1
Ball, Joseph	8bf	13	McMan, George	5	11
Ball, Peter	8bf	13	McMillan, Neil	S	7
Ball, Wesley	8bf	12	McNabb, Alex	N	8
Belfry, George	6	12	Maughn, William	5	11
Belfry, Jacob	7	11	Montgomery, S. L.	R	4
Belfrey, Sherman	6	11	Moore, Aud	6	6
Bressette, Paul	9bf	15	Robinson, James	7	7
Bressette, Theopole	7	15	Sallows, Benj.	7	11
Burzie, Charles Sr.	7	13	Sallows, Reuben	7	10
Casselman, William	E	9	Stephens, Jos.	S	13
Crooke, Ed	6	10	Sykes, Charles	S	7
Crooke, George	3	8	Taylor, William	5	9
Crooke, William	6	10	Vasey, M.	S	6
Dalton, John	6	7	Vasey, Richard	S	6
Dilling, John	S	4	Vent, A.	8	14
Eplett, J. A.	W	1	Vent, Charles	S	9
Fraser, Alex	8bf	14	Vent, Edwin	6	11
Graham, William	6	7	Vent, George	6	13
Heels, Richard	S	9	Webb, Henry	7	3
Humphries, R.	5	12	Webb, John	7	3
Hutchson, John	5	10	Webb, T. H.	6	7
Kelly, J. N.	7	7	Webb, William Jr.	6	3
Kent, George	6	12	Webb, William Sr.	6	3
Kirkwood, Robert	6	6	White, Isaac	7	10
Law, E. M. M.	S	1	Wilson, J. N.	3	12
Lile, Enoch	J	10	Wilson, R. J.	3	12
McDermitt, Angus	R	6	Winfield, John	7	12
McDowell, Jos.	5	10			

Looking north on Albert Street as a new-fangled horseless carriage roars up the road at the dizzying speed of 15 miles per hour. To the right are Ball's Drugstore, Rumball's Hardware and Jim Bernie's Jewellers Shop. One old-time resident recalls the arrival of automobiles: "Hell, they scared the horses half to death with all the racket they made, but at least they never dirtied up the roads the way the horses did." Photo c.1911.

List of Businesses 1901 & 1910

According to *Farmers' and Business Directory*, the population of Victoria Harbour was 275 in 1901.

Simcoe County Directory 1901

Anderson Fish Company
Ball, Samuel - Shoemaker
Ball, W. N. - Baker
Brown, E. - Blacksmith
Burnie, James - Jeweller
Eplett, J. A. - Butcher
Hastings, James - Hardware
Hill Brothers - General Store
McDermitt, John - Sawmill
Newton and Son - Lumber
Noble, W. N. -Baker
Northern Mercantile Co. Ltd. - General Store
Reid, Samuel - General Store
Robbins, Daniel - Hotel Keeper
Sykes, Charles - Grocer
Thorburn, Arch - Tailor
Vasey, Mark - Post Master
Vent, H. A. - General Store
Victoria Harbour Lumber Company
Weaver, C. A. - Drugstore
Wilson, Henry - Confectionery
Wismer, J. H. - Nurseryman

By 1910 nineteen more businesses were operating in the village:

Arbour, N. - Butcher
Bourgeoise, E. - Livery
Bourril, E. - Livery
Brown, T. W. - Druggist
Brown, W. E. - Physician
Burns, Sherman - Contractor
Capestrand, Joseph - Tailor
Carley, Joseph -Harnessmaker
Evans, Samuel - Blacksmith
Ferguson, W. E. N. - Blacksmith
Gamma, Edward - Butcher
Gardiner, H. L. - Photographer
Gowans, Thomas -Printer
Hinks, T. W. - Shoemaker
Lee, Sam - Hand Laundry
Livingstone, J. - Shoe Store
Patterson, Walter - Surveyor
Rumball, W. H. - Furniture & Hardware Store
Standard Bank of Canada

102

The New Era

VOL. 5. NO. 25   VICTORIA HARBOR, ONT., JUNE 5th, 1919   F. J. BAKER, Publisher

Local and General

Victoria Harbor Band open for engagements. J. Wilson, Conductor ; J. E. Stafield, Secretary.

St. Paul's Women's Missionary Society will meet at the home of Miss Margaret Schissler on Wednesday, June 11th, at 3 o'clock.

Arrangements are being made for a summer speaker in Victoria Harbor. All the ladies and girls in the vicinity are cordially invited to attend. Further announcements next week.

Rev. A. E. Neilly, B.A., of St. Paul's church, left Wednesday afternoon for Hamilton to be present at the meeting of the Presbyterian General Assembly. He was accompanied by Mrs. Neilly. They will be absent this week and next.

Mrs. W. Long, Mrs. R. Delehay and Mrs. W. Dunlop attended the annual convention of East Simcoe District Women's Institute at Orillia on Thursday, June 5th, as delegates from Victoria Harbor Branch.

The N. S. H. Club, an organization of young ladies from Newtonville, who are bent on getting all the fun out of life possible, gave a dance in the Orange Hall, on Friday night, the guests being mostly the wearers of the overseas button. There

LOST

In Victoria Harbor, on Wednesday, June 4th, a small strap purse, containing money order for $38.00, five or six $1.00 bills, and Registration Card. Finder will be rewarded by returning same to the New Era office.

For Sale.

Holstein cow, 6 years old, fresh 8 weeks. Quiet and easy milker. For particulars apply to
ROBERT MOORE,
Victoria Harbor, Ont.

For Sale.

1—31 foot glass cabin boat, 18 to 20 h.p. Cheap for cash. Small boat taken in part payment. Apply at The New Era office.

---

was a goodly company present to enjoy the dancing, and discuss the epicurean contents of sundry mysterious baskets, that found their way to the hall, and later charmed gallant heart to fair ladye. We understand this is the second of a series of these events.

We are very pleased to report that Mr. W. B. Crooke, who recently underwent a serious operation at a Toronto hospital, with serious complications developing, is now out of danger, and we hope to see him back again soon, fully restored to health.

Mr. Ewart Vasey, who was a member of the 3rd Canadian Siege Battery during the late war, now living in Montreal, is one of the fortunate ones to receive an invitation from the Julius Richardson Chapter of the I.O.D.E., to spend the summer at their camp at Chateauguay, Que. The invitation is extended to all members of the Battery.

Mrs. E. P. Vasey entertained the Ladies' Aid Societies of Ebenezer and Victoria Harbor, at her home on Wednesday, June 4th. After the general business was transacted, a dainty lunch was served by the hostess. The sincere thanks of the visiting ladies is extended to Mrs. Vasey, whose home has always been a favorite place for such assemblies.

During the war, an old Victoria Harbor boy was promoted from Captain to the rank of Major, and was also awarded the Air Service Cross, and the French Croix de Guerre. We refer to Major George M. Turnbull, who will be well remembered by many of our townspeople. Before the war, Major Turnbull was connected with the Great West Life, at Edmonton, Alta. He enlisted in the R. A. F.

The Canadian Martyr's Shrine.

The summer pilgrimage to the Shrine of the Canadian Martyrs, near Waubaushene, Ont., will be re-opened during the summer. Sometime of July and opening to take place on July 1st, and pilgrims who desire to honor the heroic missionaries who were slain by the Iroquois in the seventeenth century, will be received there as in former years.

Summer Service Opened.

The Canadian Pacific Railway last Saturday inaugurated its summer service to the West, via the Great Lakes : the Assiniboia carrying the first passengers from Port McNicoll, following the arrival of the steamboat express from Toronto at 5.15 p.m. The sailings westbound will be on Wednesday and Saturday, at 5.30 p.m. arriving Mondays and Fridays at 8 o'-clock a. m. The Manitoba will serve Owen Sound leaving that port at 10.30 p. m. each Monday.

Never in the history of the Port was the service opened under more ideal conditions. The weather the past week has been worthy of July, and the water has been placid as the proverbial mill pond being the only cool spot where existence could be endured. A heavy haze has hung over the lake in the morning and evening, and there have been sunsets of striking picturesqueness, and sublime grandeur. It is yet early June and under such ideal conditions we may expect the cry : "Here comes the bride."

ALGAR—REYNOLDS

A very pretty wedding was solemnized at the residence of the bride's father, Mr. John J. Reynolds, Victoria Harbor, at half-past eleven o'clock, on Wednesday morning, June 4th, when Lulu Mae, the eldest daughter, became the bride of Mr. Harry E. Algar of Lindsay, a popular fireman on the G.T.R. The ceremony was performed by Rev. A. J G. Carscadden, and was witnessed by a number of friends of both parties. The bride was attended by her sister, Miss Mary Reynolds, Mr. Walter Algar, brother of the groom, officiating as best man.

The bride looked charming in a dress of pink silk crepe de chene with Georgette crepe, her travelling suit being of navy blue taffeta.

After the ceremony the guests sat down to a dainty wedding luncheon, and left on the G.T.R. afternoon train for N. York City, on a short honeymoon, after which a star will be set up in the whither the very best wishes of many Victoria Harbor friends will follow them.

The bride had always been a very active member of the Choir and Y.L.B.C. of the Methodist Church, and as a farewell gift from her fellow-workers in these

---

HONOR ROLL.

Standing of Pupils in Port McNicoll Public School for May

ROOM 1.
Sr. Primer Margurite Terry, Keith Armstrong, Hugh Nex, Doris Nev, Arthur Parent, Mary Macdonald. Jr. Primer Jean McgGoe, Gordon Fraxey, Anna Reveir, Bernadetta McVeigh.

H. Ralston, teacher.

A. H. Vent's dry goods store, seen here c.1890s, was once situated on William Street. —COURTESY MRS. EPLETT

The Orange Hall was built on Albert Street at the turn of the century. On January 4, 1900, the L.O.L. elected the following officers for that year: Brothers Jas. Stewart, W.M.; Joseph Beefry, D.M.; Albert Brown, Chap.; Joseph Stephens, Rec. Sec.; W. Crooke, Fin. Sec.; George Crooke, Treasurer; R. W. Ney, Let.; W. Evans, D. of C.; William McDowell, William Ney, W. Dunlop, R. Ney and Jas. Wilson, committee. For many years the old Orange Hall was the scene of dances, card parties, socials, musicals and plays. Photo c.1915. —COURTESY MRS. BRUCE EPLETT

COMING ! COMING

Orange Hall, Victoria Harbor

WEDNESDAY

November 27th, 1918

MYSTERIOUS

MYSTO

Company

C. Cripps and C. B. Nayler. Introducing Magic, Music, Mystery and Singing. Illusion Comedy. Assisted by Roma, the Girl of Mystery, demonstrating the wonders of Second sight, Telepathy and Mind-reading.

Mandolin---MUSIC---Hawaiian

Between Acts, **WILL MARR**, one of Canada's Cleverest Comedians, will provide entertainment.

Reserved Seats, 50 and 75c.   Rush Seats, 25c.

Reserved Seat Plan at T. W. BROWN'S DRUG STORE

The Bank of Toronto under construction c. 1900.

Some Well-known Villagers
from the Past

Edward Bryon Brown, VILLAGE CLERK

Prior to his appointment on January 9, 1911, as the first offical clerk for the village of Victoria Harbour, E. B. Brown worked for several years as an engineer on the tugs. His wife, Mary-Jane, filled in as clerk that year while her husband wound up his affairs and saw to the construction of their new home on George Street. For several more years E. B. Brown also served as the village magistrate. He died in 1939 after serving as clerk for twenty-eight years.

James Heels, RAILROADER

James Heels was born in Leicestershire, England, in 1830. He began his railroad career at the tender age of nine, toting tools for the blacksmith, a job he did for seventeen years. At the age of twenty-three, in 1853, James was among the many hundreds of British men recruited to come to Canada to help construct a new railway line from Montreal to Toronto. Later, in 1879, when an extension was built by the Grand Trunk to Midland, James and his wife, Sarah Crawford, and their children relocated there. He worked as a sectionman in Victoria Harbour. After sixty-two years as a railroader, James retired in 1901. He died five years later, leaving four daughters and six sons—James, Peter, Richard, William, Joseph, and Harry—all of whom followed in their father's footsteps.

Christopher Burns, VILLAGE CARPENTER

Chris Burns was born in Lafroy and came to the village with his family in the 1880s at the age of twelve. His father, Samuel, a carpenter, taught young Chris the building trade, and together they were responsible for the construction of many of the homes and buildings that remain in the village today, including St. John's United Church. Chris and his wife, Jane Rumney, raised two sons and three daughters in Victoria Harbour: Wallace, Ivan, Gladys, Bernice and Marjory. Mr. Burns was active in both the community and the church. He also served on the council and was a member of the Oddfellows and treasurer of the Triple Link Lodge. He passed away in February 1932. His daughter Marjory worked at the *New Era* newspaper office as a typesetter before her marriage to Gordon Gervia in Toronto in 1928. Gordon was employed by the C.P.R. as chief engineer on the *Keewatin.*

Henry LaBatt

Born on an Indian Reserve at Britt, Ontario, Henry LaBatt was the eldest of twelve children. At the age of thirteen he went to work at the Victoria Harbour Lumber Company on the Boardway, and several years later he was employed as a lumberjack. In 1920 he worked for a dredging firm as a driller, and later for the C.P.R. On August 13, 1937, his home on William Street was levelled by a fire which also destroyed the Catholic Church and several other homes.

Florence Brown Belcher, FORMER REEVE

Florence Brown is the daughter of E. B. Brown. One of her first jobs was in the *New Era* newspaper office, located where the firehall stands today. She later worked in the telephone office, located behind the old company store. Before and after her marriage to Captain Reginald Belcher, Florence had a keen interest in civic affairs. In 1955 Florence became the first woman Reeve in Simcoe County, a position she held for two years. Thirty-one years later Mrs. Belcher still manages to attend meetings on a regular basis.

Duncan MacKenzie, VILLAGE PHYSICIAN

Duncan MacKenzie was born in Kirkfield, Ontario, in 1882, the third son in a family of four boys and a girl. He graduated from the University of Toronto in 1907 and arrived in Victoria Harbour seven years later, in August 1914, to assume the position of practitioner from Dr. W. E. Brown.

His practice was far-flung, and during those early days he made his rounds by automobile, horse and cutter, and sometimes by dogsled. His house calls often resulted in overnight stays.

Duncan married schoolteacher Frances Smyth, the youngest daughter of Job and Catherine Smyth. The Smyths had come to Victoria Harbour in 1900, Job accepting the position of manager at the Victoria Harbour Lumber Company's lath mill. Frances obtained her teaching certificate from the Toronto Normal School.

Duncan and Frances wed in 1920 and took up residence with the Smyths in a house on the northwest corner of Richard and Ellen streets. The front parlours were turned into an office and waiting room.

The MacKenzies had four children: Ewen, an engineering draftsman who today occupies the old family home; Alexander, who practises medicine in Penetanguishene; John, also a physician, who resides in Elmvale; and Catherine, a Victoria Harbour resident who is active in civic affairs and a member of the Local Architectural Conservation Advisory Committee.

The autumn before his death in 1965, Dr. Duncan MacKenzie was honoured by the townspeople of Victoria Harbour for his fifty years of dedicated service to the village.

Did You Know . . .

— the first meeting of the council for the village was held on the ninth day of January 1911 at 11 a.m.?

— James M. Gill was Reeve and J. Schissler, A. Thorburn, N. Arbour, Felix LaBatte, councillors, E. Bryon Brown, clerk?

— that in 1912 the new chief constable and road-overseer was allotted a salary of $600 a year? Mr. Fergeson's new uniform cost taxpayers $30.10?

— at one time Eplett's Butcher Shop was used as a temporary school?

— the printer's office was first located in Rumball's Store, type was set by hand and the average wage was $6 a week in the 1920s?

— the present-day Senior Citizens building was once the warehouse for Billy Reid's Store?

— St. Mary's Church is built on the former site of a dance hall?

— a tennis court was once situated behind St. Paul's Church on Ellen?

— after the mills closed down in 1927 the millworkers' cottages could be purchased for as little as $100?

— from the turn of the century until the 1920s many residents had maids, housekeepers and cooks?

— the publisher of the *New Era* newspaper (1916) was Athol McQuarrie?

— there was once a widow's watch on the roof of the Victoria Manor and it is believed to have housed a telescope?

— around the turn of the century the Women's Institute held their meetings in the dining room of the Royal Victoria Hotel?

— on the day that the village received their new fire truck (a 1919 LaFrance) members of town council drove to Toronto to pick it up. On the way home the members of council followed the fire truck rather closely through the streets of Toronto so as not to lose sight of their new truck. A few days later a summons was sent to the owner of the car (we won't mention his name), charging him with following too close behind a fire truck?

— before purchasing their first fire truck, the auxiliary pump and big hose reel were towed behind a half-ton pickup truck?

— the firehall was once a chicken factory, and before that a church?

— on November 19, 1918, it was recorded that the village post office sold a record number of stamps, $34 worth?

— the original library desk used in 1916 was traced to Waubaushene Public Library?

At the corner of Albert and Richard streets.

—COURTESY MRS. EPLETT

Moments in Time

MORE THAN SEVENTY-SEVEN years ago Victoria Harbour was one of the busiest and most prosperous villages in Simcoe County. Ships both large and small plied Hogg's Bay and steam engines pulled a string of freight and passenger coaches through daily. The inevitable excitement of arrival and departure, loading and unloading created a constant scene of hustle and bustle along the waterfront.

Workers in rough clothes and loggers in flannel shirts and stagged-off pants stepped lively between the mills and the wharf, their voices a curious blend of many accents.

On any given day the roads south of the mills were clogged with farmers' wagons, merchants' drays and gentry's buggies. Rough-planked boardwalks and wood-framed storefronts lined the dusty streets. Shopkeepers in long white aprons helped housewives with parcels to waiting carriages. Gentlemen in bowler hats and vested suits with gold watch chains nodded in passing to ladies in long skirts and wide-brimmed hats. Salesmen with bulging sample cases discussed their wares over counters with prospective buyers. Out in the street clouds of dust whirled in the air when one of the village's few automobiles coughed and choked and jockeyed for position near the dancing hooves of a nervous mare. A bicycle darted through the melee, expertly dodging a team of Clydesdales being led up the road to the

A twelve-horse team—count them—used to plough the village streets c.1915.
—COURTESY
THEO BERNARD

company stables on Albert Street. Everywhere the sights and sounds of a thriving mill town were evident.

The village was laid out south, east and west of the bay. The homes of the millworkers were interspersed with those of other working-class residents. The village elite, prosperous merchants, company managers and foremen, the doctor, the banker, the pharmacist, retired laker captains and a judge built their neat two-storey brick and rambling clapboard houses up the hill south of William Street. Shady side porches and wrap-around verandahs adorned with yards of gingerbread trim and trailing vines of honeysuckle and clematis provided cozy retreats on sultry summer evenings.

Almost every home had a vegetable patch out back and a flower garden where hollyhocks, peonies and roses bloomed in wild profusion behind a cedar hedge or picket fence with a swinging garden gate. Tall maples lined dirt roads, creating a shady canopy of shimmering green. An air of tranquility prevailed, with only the sound of a dog barking off in the distance, the occasional slamming of an old screen door or the creaking wheels of a carriage as it rolled along the gravel road.

Over several decades of long, languid summer days, village photographer Harry L. Gardiner captured forever the stiff faces and self-conscious poses of villagers at weddings, picnics, parades and in

"Horse and Buggy Days". A Sunday afternoon outing along William Street c.1910. —COURTESY CLARENCE SYKES

family portraits. Wonderful sepia prints depict every facet of village life around the turn of the century—its people, its streets and its architecture, an indelible record of that golden era.

There were concerts and plays, Sunday School picnics, dances, vigorous games of tennis on the courts behind St. Paul's, and memorable moonlight cruises out on the bay. There were afternoon luncheons in the dining room at the Royal Victoria Hotel, and tea parties and strawberry socials in the front parlours of the village ladies. On such occasions Irish linen and fancy handmade lace tablecloths were brought out, along with their best china, silver tea sets and servers. The ladies wore their best broadcloth and linen skirts topped with their finest lace-trimmed lawn shirt-waists. Their adornment was simple, a cameo brooch, a jet filigree necklace, or an ornate watch fob pinned to their bodice. Their hats were worn with pride, elaborate confections liberally garnished with delicate satin roses, ribbons and bows. The more daring sported colourful plumes of garish feathers with a little bird or two perched in a bed of lace. Beyond the garden gate the sounds of lighthearted laughter and tinkling teacups could be heard by passers-by.

Like images on those faded sepia photographs, time stands still as we remember those days long ago—the quiet ticking of a mantel clock in the front parlor, the creaking of grandpa's rocker out on the back porch, the wonderful aroma of burning autumn leaves in the back yard, the haunting whistle of a steam engine as it passes through town at dusk—memories of our old home town, a mill town, Victoria Harbour, Ontario.

Vera and Harry Rumney, taken at Gardiner's Studio, Victoria Harbour.   —COURTESY VERA BOYER

Going to the Coldwater Fair was a big event, as is evident in this turn-of-the-century photograph. Note the iron wood-burner at No. 2 mill in the background. In the left foreground is Gardiner's Studio. Note the skylights. The brick house was once Mrs. Burnier's Millinery shop. It later became the Bank of Toronto. This photo was taken from the corner of William and Albert streets. —COURTESY OF MARY EPLETT

"The Good Old Summertime". A young lad fishes with a long pole as his mother, aunt and little sister look on from the Red Bridge over the Hogg River c.1890s.
—COURTESY MARY GERMAIN

Dexter's Grove, Victoria Harbor, Ont.

Dexter's Grove in the Harbour was a favourite camping spot for tourists around the 1900s. —COURTESY CLARENCE SYKES

Sunday School picnic c.1900.   —COURTESY VERA BOYER

John Eplett (in striped apron) poses outside his meat market on Albert Street south of William. Note the sides of beef brought out especially for the photo. To the left are the lumber company stables. This photo c.1900.

—COURTESY MRS. EPLETT

The Lumberjack

BEN SCHELLE
author of "Earth Feelings"

There are twisted trails that take you, to the places that I've seen;
ragged routes that follow rivers in decline.
And I knew these roads of yesteryear, and all that land of green;
when I worked my trade among the giant pine.

For I was a rugged logger when the pine grew thick and tall,
and I know I helped to bring about their end.
But we thought they'd grow forever, so we hurled them every fall,
with the hope of finally having cash to spend.

Oh it was a different time then when this land was newly won,
and a homestead was a fragile thing to own.
So we menfolk left our women, once the harvesting was done,
and hiked to where the pine were overgrown.

Then the building of the tote-roads, and the camp and the depot;
and the cutting of the pine trees into logs.
'Till we skidded them to rollways, piled and waiting for the snow;
and the sleighs to haul them off like butchered hogs.

Haul them down the snowy sleigh trails, to the frozen river ice,
there to wait until the season of the thaw.
When we'd have to take the gamble, like a careless toss of dice,
to see who could obey the river law.

For the river was the ruler, when we rode her back,
and she called the shots which we were quick to heed.
With her cataracts and rapids, she could cure a lumberjack,
and I've seen her even tame the toughest Swede.

I recall the days of driving as a challenge and a spree,
as we danced with pike poles on the bobbing bark.
For we all were young and able, and the river made us free,
with its waters racing wild and deep and dark.

But the river ride was over once we dumped into the lake,
where the logs were circled by a timber boom.
Then they moved by pulse of piston, or then if the winds were great,
we would drift them to the mill and to their doom.

Oh the mill towns they were something, quite impressive to us boys,
who were used to camps and homesteads in the wood.
For the buildings and machinery, the smokestacks and the noise,
seemed a strange place to attain a livelyhood.

Some were tempted by the challenge, others by the steady pay;
yet most didn't last a month around a mill.
For the forests and the freedom, seemed to lure the men away;
loggers like to know what lies beyond the hill.

Bibliography

Books

Craig, John. *The Recent Past.* Simcoe, Ontario:
  Corporation of the County of Simcoe, 1977.

Heels, Charles H. *Railroad Recollections.*
  Museum Restoration Service, 1980.

Hunter, Andrew F. *A History of Simcoe County.*
  Barrie, Ontario: Barrie County Council, 1909.

Leitch, Adelaide. *The Visible Past, County of Simcoe.*
  Toronto: Ryerson Press, 1967.

Witney, Dudley. *The Lighthouse.* Toronto:
  McClelland and Stewart, 1975.

Newspapers

Victoria Harbour *New Era,*
  editions from 1914, 1918 and 1919.

Barrie *Northern Advance.*

Midland *Free Press Herald.*

Midland *County Herald.*

Midland *Free Press.*

The Midland Argus.

Orillia *Expositor.*

Toronto *Globe.*

Toronto *Star.*

Toronto *World.*

Reports

Canadian Department of Marine and Fisheries
  annual reports, 1910-1912.

Maps

Insurance Map of Victoria Harbour, 1890,
  Simcoe County Archives.

Libraries & Archives

Barrie Public Library.

Huronia Historical Parks Resource Centre.

Metropolitan Toronto Reference Library.

Midland Public Library.

Simcoe County Archives.

About the Authors

BARBARANNE BOYER-BRUYNSON was born in England and came to Canada with her English mother and Canadian father in 1946, when they returned to her father's hometown of Victoria Harbour. The family soon moved to Toronto, but Barbaranne spent most of her childhood summers at her grandmother's home in "The Harbour" and later in Muskoka, where the discovery of abandoned homesteads led to an interest in Ontario's history. In 1985 she wrote *The Boardwalk Album: Memories of The Beach*, followed in 1987 by *Muskoka's Grand Hotels* (both published by The Boston Mills Press). She is currently working on her fourth book and concluding research for her first novel at her home in Belleville, Ontario.

MICHAEL A. BOYER was born in Toronto in 1958, the youngest of the four Boyer children. His avid interest in the preservation of Ontario's marine heritage began several years ago while researching Toronto's waterfront district. Today he has a growing collection of both vintage postcards and photographs of many of Ontario's old lighthouses and railway stations. He is presently researching the Georgian Bay region for a second book. Michael lives with his wife, Yvonne, near Bowmanville, Ontario.

Index